CZECH REPUBLIC TRAVEL GUIDE

Prague, Bohemia, Český, Krumlov, Karlovy, Vary, Plzeň, Moravia, Brno, Olomouc, and Mikulov

All rights reserved. No part of this publication may be reproduced, distributed, or transmitted in any form or by any means, including photocopying, recording, or other electronic or mechanical methods, without the prior written permission of the publisher, except in the case of brief quotations embodied in critical reviews and certain other noncommercial uses permitted by copyright law.
Copyright ©Anthony Guide, 2023.

TABLE OF CONTENT

CHAPTER 1
    Introduction to the Czech Republic
    Overview of the nation
    Background History

CHAPTER 2
    Important Information for Travelers
    Travel Planning and Preparation
    Information on Entry Requirements and Visas
    Banking and Money
    Czech transportation system

CHAPTER 3
    Exploring Prague
    Overview of Prague
    Must-Go Places to Visit in Prague
    Charles Bridge and Prague Castle
    The Astronomical Clock and Old Town Square
    Lesser Town and Petn Hill
    Cultural Organizations, Museums, and Galleries
    Nightlife and Dining in Prague

CHAPTER 4
    Learning about Czech Regions
    Bohemia
    Český Krumlov
    Karlovy Vary

    Plzeň
    Moravia
    Brno
    Olomouc
    Mikulov
Additional Important Areas
    Mountains of Beskydy
    Bohemia North

CHAPTER 5
    Bohemian Paradise
    Šumava National Park
    National Park of Krkonoše
    Adršpach-Teplice Rocks
    Trails for biking and hiking
    Winter activities and water sports

CHAPTER 6
    Czech food and traditional treats
    Customary Czech Food
    Well-known Czech brews and beers
    Wine Region Areas and Tasting Opportunities
    Local Food Markets and Festivals

CHAPTER 7
    Cultural Events and Holidays
    Czech performing arts and music
    Local customs and attire
    Christmas celebrations and markets
    Easter traditions and celebrations
    Film Festivals and Other Cultural Attractions

CHAPTER 8
    Practical Advice and Safety Recommendations
    Information on health and safety
    Regional Customs and Protocol
    Common Expressions and Czech Words
    Buying goods and souvenirs
    Traveling with Kids or Pets

CHAPTER 9
    Recommendations for Day Trips and Itineraries
    Day Trips from Prague
    Multi-day Routes for Country Exploration

CHAPTER 10
    Options for Accommodation
    Tour Guides and Transportation Services

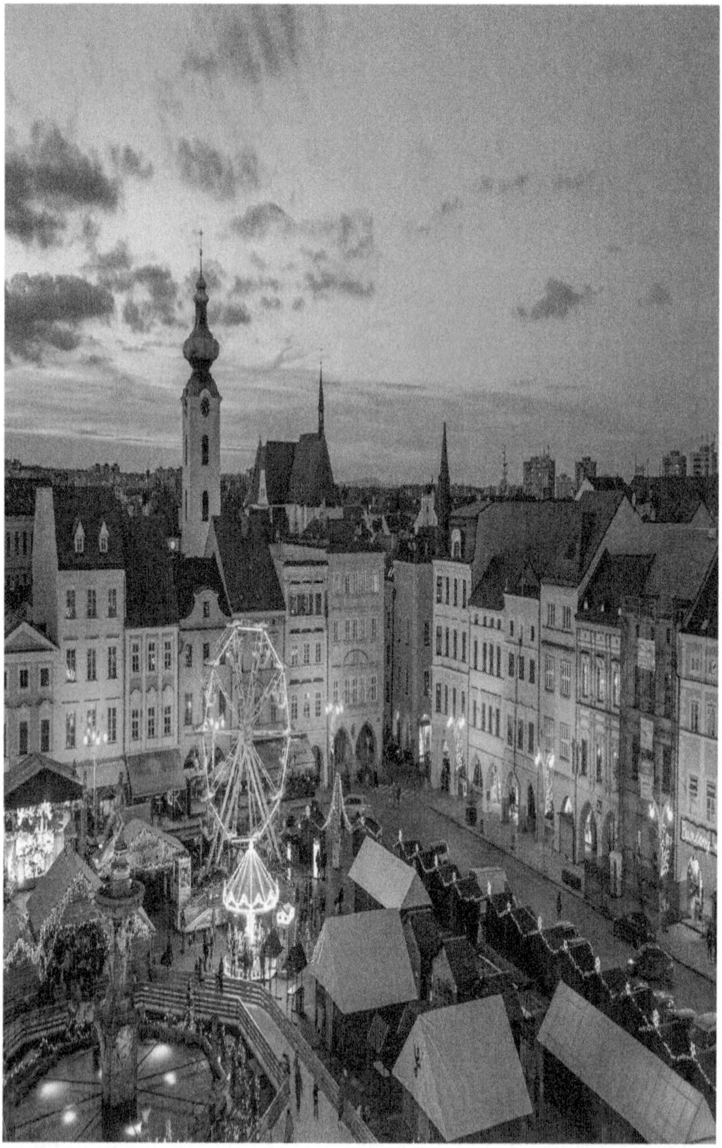

CHAPTER 1

Introduction to the Czech Republic

Learn about the Czech Republic, an intriguing nation tucked away in the center of Europe, and its stunning beauty and fascinating history. This guide is your key to uncovering the wonders of this amazing location, from the fairy-tale charm of Prague to the breathtaking landscapes of Bohemia and Moravia. Take in all of Prague's splendor, including its imposing castles, complex architecture, and thriving cultural scene. Discover the flavors of traditional Czech food, take in the energy of bustling markets, and stroll through the winding cobblestone alleyways. Explore Bohemia and Moravia's hidden gems outside of the city to find intriguing villages, breathtaking national parks, and age-old castles.

The Czech Republic provides a wide range of experiences to fit any traveler's preferences, whether you're an outdoor enthusiast looking for adventure in nature, a history buff exploring the past, or a lover of art and culture immersing yourself in the vibrant environment.

This travel book is your traveling companion, offering crucial knowledge, insider advice, and suggestions to make your trip special. Learn about the must-see sights, get a taste of the local food, learn about customs and traditions, and get useful tips for navigating the nation.
So be ready for an exciting adventure through the Czech Republic, where history, culture, and stunning natural scenery all come together to make for a genuinely unique travel experience. Let this book serve as your ticket to an exciting journey across this mysterious nation.

Overview of the nation

The Czech Republic, a landlocked nation in Central Europe, is bordered to the west by Germany, to the south by Austria, to the east by Slovakia, and the northeast by Poland. The Czech Republic is an intriguing location that provides a wide variety of activities. It has a rich history, beautiful architecture, and spectacular landscapes. The nation is well-known for its enchanting capital city of Prague, also known as the "City of a Hundred Spires." Prague's architecture, which includes the recognizable Prague Castle, Charles Bridge, and the Astronomical Clock in the Old Town Square, is a stunning fusion of Gothic, Renaissance, and Baroque styles. The city is a favorite destination for tourists because of its cobblestone alleys, busy markets, and lively ambiance.

The Czech Republic is known for its scenic countryside and old towns outside of Prague. Bohemia and Moravia are filled with picturesque countryside, quaint spa towns, and medieval castles. The well-preserved medieval town of Esk Krumlov, a UNESCO World Heritage site, charms tourists, whilst Karlovy

Vary is well-known for its warm springs and opulent architecture.

The national parks and natural treasures of the Czech Republic will satisfy nature lovers. Opportunities can be found at Bohemian Paradise, Umava National Park, and the Krkonoe Mountains. for stunning scenery exploration, cycling, and hiking. The nation is renowned for its abundance of rivers and lakes that are perfect for water sports aficionados, as well as its network of well-maintained bicycle paths.

With a focus on literature, music, and the arts, the Czech Republic has a rich cultural past. The nation has given world-renowned composers like Antonn Dvoák and Bedich Smetana, and it often holds festivals and other cultural events. Traditional folk festivals and rituals are treasured and observed, providing a window into the colorful traditions and customs of the nation.

Goulash, svková (marinated beef in a creamy sauce), and trdelnak (a sweet pastry) are typical dishes from the substantial and rich Czech cuisine. The nation is also renowned for its well-established beer culture, which boasts a huge selection of top-notch beers to try and a lengthy history of brewing.

The Czech Republic is a travel destination that appeals to all types of tourists because of its enthralling history, magnificent architecture, gorgeous scenery, and friendly people. Whether you want to experience a different culture, go on an outdoor adventure, or get a taste of history, this magical nation is guaranteed to make an impression.

Background History

The historical past of the Czech Republic is rich and complex, and it has shaped its identity and influenced its cultural legacy. Here is a quick rundown of significant events in Czech history:

- Early Settlements: Humans have lived in the area that is now the Czech Republic since the Stone Age. Germanic and Slavic peoples arrived in the region after the Celtic tribes.
- Great Moravia: The Great Moravian Empire became a significant nation in Central Europe in the ninth century. It

played a significant impact in the development of Christianity in the area and included portions of the modern Czech Republic, Slovakia, and Hungary.
- Bohemian Kingdom: The Pemyslid dynasty ruled the Czech territories in the 11th century, founding the Bohemian Kingdom. The capital and a major hub for political and cultural influence became Prague. During this time, the Czech lands went through periods of economic prosperity and cultural advancement.
- Hussite Movement: In the 15th century, religious reformer Jan Hus criticized Catholic Church policies, which led to the emergence of the Hussite movement. The Hussites fought against the Catholic Church and outside forces, influencing local politics and religion.
- Habsburg Rule: The Czech territories came under the rule of the Habsburg family in the 16th century, and they were included in the massive Austro-Hungarian Empire. This signaled

the end of centralized government and Vienna-inspired culture.
- Czech National Revival: In the 19th century, academics and artists led a movement to revive the Czech language, culture, and identity. The development of a sense of national pride and resistance to Germanization was greatly aided by this effort. The Czechoslovak Republic was first created in 1918, following the conclusion of World War I. It was a democratic nation that incorporated Slovakia and the Czech Republic. The new republic embraced contemporary values, experienced economic expansion, and developed into a center of cultural activity.
- World War II and the Communist Period: Nazi Germany invaded the Czech lands during World War II. Following the war, the nation was influenced by the Soviet Union, which resulted in the installation of a communist government in 1948. Up until the Velvet Revolution in 1989, the Czech Republic was a component of the

communist-run Czechoslovak Socialist Republic.
- Czech Republic and the Velvet Revolution: In 1989, the Velvet Revolution signaled a peaceful change from communism to democracy. After Václav Havel was elected as Czechoslovakia's first post-communist leader, the country peacefully divided into the Czech Republic and Slovakia in 1993.

The Czech Republic is a democratic nation today and a part of the EU. Its historical landmarks, cultural practices, and diversified legacy have all been maintained, making it a fascinating destination for visitors curious to delve into its complex past.

CHAPTER 2

Important Information for Travelers

It's crucial to be ready and knowledgeable before setting out on your vacation to the Czech Republic to make it as easy and hassle-free as possible. You will find all the necessary details and helpful advice you need in this part to plan your trip with confidence.

We've got you covered on everything from preparing for your trip to admission criteria and visa details. Learn about financial options, the local currency, and language and communication hints so you can get around efficiently. You can conveniently move around and discover the wonders of the Czech Republic by learning useful information about the country's transportation alternatives.

Your health and safety are our top priorities, and we offer vital health and safety advice as well as pointers on regional customs and etiquette to help you have a polite and pleasurable visit. Additionally, we provide helpful idioms and fundamental Czech terminology to help you communicate better with locals and make the most of your visit to this captivating nation.

To help you choose the best solutions for your trip requirements, this area includes resources and suggestions for lodging choices, transportation services, and tour operators. We cater to a range of travel interests and offer information on shopping, souvenirs, and traveling with kids or pets.

This area will be an invaluable resource for ensuring a smooth and enjoyable trip, whether you're visiting the Czech Republic for the first time or returning after a long absence. So jump right in, get the information you require, and get ready to travel to the Czech Republic for a memorable vacation!

Travel Planning and Preparation

Careful planning and preparation can help to ensure a smooth and pleasurable journey when it comes to your travel arrangements and getting ready for your vacation to the Czech Republic. Here are some basic guides to help you:

- Create a basic itinerary by first researching the most popular tourist destinations, cities, and regions in the Czech Republic. Prioritize the locations and experiences you don't want to miss and decide how long you will be there.
- Best Time to Visit: Take into account the season of the year you intend to travel. The Czech Republic has different seasons, including cool winters and gentle summers. Autumn (September to October) and spring (April to June) typically have nicer weather and fewer tourists.
- Check your country's entry regulations for details on visa needs. For stays up to 90 days, citizens of numerous nations,

including those in the EU and the US, are exempt from visa requirements. Make sure your passport is valid for at least six months after the day you intend to depart.
- The Czech koruna (CZK) is the nation of the Czech Republic's official currency. Learn about the current conversion rates and think about bringing some local money with you. Credit cards are usually accepted at most businesses, and ATMs are frequently available.
- Even though Czech is the national tongue, English is often spoken in tourist hotspots, hotels, and dining establishments. To improve your contacts with locals, it's beneficial to learn a few fundamental Czech words and pleasantries.
- Consider purchasing travel insurance to protect against unanticipated medical costs and trip cancellations. Check to see if your insurance covers the Czech Republic. It's also a good idea to find out if you need any shots before your trip.

- Transportation: Become familiar with your alternatives for getting about the Czech Republic. Public transit is well-developed and effective, including trains and buses. For limitless travel within particular areas or cities, take into account buying a transportation pass.
- Accommodations: Choose the kind of lodging you prefer and make your reservations early, especially in the busiest travel times. Luxury hotels, inexpensive hostels, and welcoming guesthouses are all available in the Czech Republic.
- Respect local customs and manners by adhering to them. Dobr den (good day) and a handshake are appropriate greetings. Rounding up the bill is a regular technique, and tipping is commonplace in restaurants.
- Make copies of all of your essential trip documents, such as your passport, travel insurance policy, and itinerary. Consider keeping digital copies on your smartphone or email, and keep the

duplicates stored apart from the originals.

You can guarantee a well-planned and stress-free vacation to the Czech Republic by adhering to this advice on travel planning and preparation. As you tour this alluring location, embrace the nation's rich history, beautiful architecture, and welcoming people.

Information on Entry Requirements and Visas

Depending on your country, the reason for your visit, and the length of your stay, the Czech Republic may have different entry requirements and visa information. For your reference, the following general information:

- Visa-Free Travel: Citizens of numerous nations, including those in the European Union, the United States, Canada, Australia, and New Zealand, are not required to get a visa to travel to the Czech Republic for up to 90 days Please be aware that these visa exemptions are subject to modification, therefore it is

always advisable to confirm the most recent rules that apply to your country of residence.
- The Czech Republic is a member of the Schengen Area, a grouping of 26 nations in Europe with no external border restrictions. You may enter the Czech Republic and other Schengen nations during the specified period if you have a valid Schengen visa.
- Valid Passport: Verify that your passport will still be valid for at least six months after the date you intend to leave the Czech Republic. Most tourists must meet this condition, however, it is advisable to confirm the particular validity criteria based on your citizenship.
- Long-Term Stay and Work: If you want to work or study while staying in the Czech Republic for more than 90 days, you may need to apply for a long-term visa or residence permit. These visas typically call for additional paperwork, such as evidence of lodging, financial stability, health insurance, and a justification for your visit. For further details and

requirements, it is advised that you contact the Czech embassy or consulate that is most conveniently located in your nation.

- How to Apply for a Visa: If you require a visa to enter the Czech Republic, you must ordinarily apply at the Czech embassy or consulate in your country. The application procedure could entail completing paperwork, supplying supporting materials, paying a fee, and going through an interview. It's crucial to give yourself enough time because applying for a visa might take weeks or even months.
- Travel insurance is strongly advised when visiting the Czech Republic even though it is not a formal entrance requirement. Make sure your insurance covers any potential mishaps during your stay, medical costs, and trip cancellation or interruption.

Banking and Money

The Czech koruna (CZK) is the nation of the Czech Republic's official currency. It's crucial to have a fundamental understanding of the local currency and banking options before visiting the Czech Republic. Here are some crucial details:

- Exchange your foreign currency for Czech koruna at banks, exchange bureaus (commonly referred to as "smnárna"), or even select hotels. Banks typically provide competitive exchange rates, however, they might only be open during certain hours. Exchange offices are more prevalent and may be found in tourist locations and airports, but because rates might vary, it is best to compare them before making an exchange.
- ATMs, often known as "bankomat," are widely distributed throughout the Czech Republic. Cash withdrawals are also possible from ATMs. Major credit and debit cards like Visa and Mastercard are accepted there. It can be practical to withdraw money in local currency using

ATMs. Check with your bank about any potential fees or limits on cash withdrawals as some ATMs may charge a fee for foreign transactions.
- Credit and Debit Cards: In larger cities and prominent tourist destinations, credit and debit cards are routinely accepted in hotels, restaurants, stores, and tourist attractions. The most widely accepted cards are Visa and Mastercard, with American Express and Discover, perhaps having a smaller acceptance range. To avoid any problems using your card, it's a good idea to let your bank know about your trip intentions.
- The normal banking hours in the Czech Republic are from 9:00 AM to 5:00 PM, Monday through Friday. Most banks are closed on Sundays and public holidays, while some may have limited hours on Saturdays. ATMs are open for cash withdrawals around-the-clock.
- For your convenience, it is advised to carry a combination of cash and credit cards. Despite the widespread acceptance of cards, it might still be helpful to have

some cash on hand for small shops, neighborhood markets, or rural places where card acceptance may be constrained. Use caution while making modest purchases with large amounts (like 2,000 CZK notes), as some stores might not have enough change.
- Safety and Security: When using ATMs or handling money, it's important to use caution and be aware of your surroundings, as with any area you visit. Use ATMs that are situated in well-lit, safe areas, and use caution when entering your PIN.
- Don't forget to let your bank know about your vacation intentions to avoid any unforeseen card troubles or blockages. Additionally, it's a good idea to keep your bank's customer support number and emergency contact information close by in case anything goes wrong with your cards or banking services.

Knowing the currency and banking alternatives available in the Czech Republic can help you decide how to best meet your financial demands while there and guarantee a simple and easy experience.

Czech transportation system

You can choose from a range of modes of transportation in the Czech Republic to let you discover the nation's cities, towns, and picturesque landscapes. The primary forms of transportation are as follows:
- Public transit: In the Czech Republic, especially in big cities like Prague, public transit is dependable, effective, and well-developed. Metro systems, trams, buses, and trains are all included. Here is a description of each:
- Metro: The A, B, and C lines of Prague's extensive metro system encompass both the city core and its surroundings. The metro is a convenient method to get around Prague, and it's especially helpful for visiting well-known tourist attractions.

- Trams and Buses: Within cities and towns, trams and buses are the main modes of transportation. They offer comprehensive coverage and are a practical way to visit various areas and attractions. Tickets can be bought at ticket machines or onboard (buses require exact change).
- Trains: In the Czech Republic, trains are a great way to go about the country's towns and countryside. The nation's well-connected rail system provides smooth and beautiful rides. Local trains, also known as "Osobn vlak," serve smaller towns and villages while high-speed trains, also known as "Rychlk," connect major cities.
- Taxis: Taxis can be hailed on the street or reserved via a phone app, and they are generally available in urban areas. It is advised to choose recognized taxi services or to request a pricing estimate before boarding the car. In large cities, ride-sharing services like Uber are available.

- Car Rental: Renting a car is an alternative if you want more freedom and flexibility. Airports and major cities are home to international vehicle rental agencies. However, be aware that driving in city centers might be difficult owing to traffic and a lack of parking. It's a good idea to become familiar with the parking and driving laws in your area.
- Cycling: The Czech Republic is noted for its attractive cycling routes, especially in rural and scenic locations, and it has a well-developed bicycle infrastructure. Major cities have bike lanes and provide bike rentals. Cycling across the countryside is a great way to take in the natural beauty of the nation.
- Domestic Flights: Due to the Czech Republic's tiny size, there aren't many domestic flights available. However, a few minor airports provide domestic connections if you need to travel vast distances swiftly.
- Travel cards: Considering travel cards for unlimited travel inside particular regions or cities may be worthwhile depending on

your travel schedule. These passes can save you money, especially if you intend to use public transportation frequently.

In general, the Czech Republic has a well-connected and effective transportation system that makes it simple to travel around the nation. You will have options that suit your preferences and assist you in navigating this lovely place, whether you decide to take public transportation, taxis, rental cars, or bicycles.

CHAPTER 3

Exploring Prague

Welcome to Prague, the charming Czech Republic's capital! Prague, a city teeming with history, culture, and stunning architecture, is nestled along the banks of the Vltava River. The city of Prague offers an enthralling fusion of traditional charm and contemporary life, from its medieval Old Town to the majesty of Prague Castle.

A breathtaking landscape of Gothic spires, Baroque facades, and Art Nouveau decorations will greet you as you explore Prague. Explore stunning cathedrals, get lost in the winding cobblestone alleyways, and wander across charming bridges. Don't miss to enjoy the astronomical marvels of the famous Astronomical Clock in Old Town Square as well as the spectacular views from the famous Charles Bridge.

Explore Prague's thriving cultural scene, which is home to top-notch theaters, galleries, and museums. The city's artistic tradition is alive and well, with everything from avant-garde performances to concerts of classical music. Enjoy substantial meals like goulash, dumplings, and traditional Czech beer that make up Czech cuisine.

Prague's areas outside of the historical center have their special attractions. Explore the hip pubs and galleries in Ikov, meander through the quaint alleyways of Malá Strana, or retreat to Petn Hill's lush refuge. Also, don't pass up the chance to explore Prague's nightlife, which features exciting clubs, inviting pubs, and rooftop bars with breathtaking views of the city's lit-up cityscape.

Prague cordially invites you to explore its fascinating past, awe at its magnificent architecture, and experience the friendly hospitality of its residents. Prague guarantees an amazing experience, whether you're a history aficionado, an art lover, a foodie, or just an inquisitive tourist.

Prepare to be enchanted by Prague's enchanting ambiance, where centuries of history and contemporary allure converge to create a place that will live in your heart forever. Prepare to set off on an exciting voyage as you discover this Central European treasure.

Overview of Prague

Welcome to Prague, the Czech Republic's capital and a genuine gem of Europe! Prague is a city that seamlessly combines the old and the new, enticing people from all over the world with its stunning architecture and history.

You will travel back in time as you stroll through Prague's narrow streets. The city's well-preserved medieval structures, Gothic cathedrals, and picturesque cobblestone pathways bring its extensive past to life. Every part of Prague has a tale to tell, from the recognizable Prague Castle sitting on a hill overlooking the city to the spectacular Charles Bridge ornamented with statues and busy with street performers.

Take in the lovely ambiance of the Old Town Square, where the ornate Astronomical Clock and the Gothic spires of the Tn Church provide a stunning scene. Enjoy the expansive views of Prague's skyline, accented by the imposing

Prague Castle and the elegant Charles Bridge, while taking a stroll along the Vltava River.

Prague is a bustling center of culture in addition to being a city of incredible architectural treasures. A lively arts culture is on display at the city's theaters, concert venues, and galleries, which host performances and exhibitions of everything from classic classics to cutting-edge modern works. Explore the writings, music, and artwork of renowned Czech authors, composers, and artists who have made a lasting impact on culture.

You'll learn about the distinctive personalities and undiscovered gems of Prague's neighborhoods as you explore them. Each neighborhood has its unique flavor and ambiance, from the bohemian attitude of Ikov to the romantic allure of Malá Strana. Try hearty delicacies like goulash, svková, and trdelnk while indulging in authentic Czech cuisine and world-famous Czech beer.

Prague's appeal goes far beyond its historical and artistic attractions. Its vibrant nightlife scene offers something for everyone, from hip clubs and busy bars to cozy pubs hidden away in old cellars. As you mix with locals and other travelers, enjoy a night of music, dance, and celebration.

Be prepared to be mesmerized by the timeless beauty, warm ambiance, and feeling of history that characterize Prague's cobblestone streets. Prague guarantees a memorable experience that will have you itching to come back repeatedly, whether you're visiting its famous buildings, indulging in its delectable cuisine, or simply getting lost in its romantic atmosphere.

Must-Go Places to Visit in Prague

Several must-see sights in Prague highlight the city's extensive history, stunning architecture, and cultural relevance. The following are some of the top sights you ought to have on your itinerary:

Charles Bridge and Prague Castle

Two famous sites that you must see when in Prague are Prague Castle and Charles Bridge. Let's examine these amazing sights in more detail:
- Prague Castle is a vast complex that dominates the city's skyline and has been a part of more than a thousand years of Czech history. It is the world's greatest complex of old castles and is filled with magnificent architecture, priceless artifacts, and amazing views.

- St. Vitus church is a spectacular Gothic church that stands out in Prague Castle and is a work of art with complex features, towering spires, and breathtaking stained glass windows. Learn more about its opulent interior, which features the majestic St. Wenceslas Chapel.
- Golden Lane: Wander along this quaint street surrounded by vibrant homes to experience a step back in time. It provides a window into the life of the prior occupants of the castle, including famed Czech author Franz Kafka.
- Visit the former residence of Czech kings and presidents at the Old Royal Palace. Discover the magnificent Vladislav Hall, a sizable Gothic hall used for significant occasions, as well as the royal chambers.
- Changing of the Guard: View the hourly ceremony of the changing of the guard at the castle's main entrance. The sight of the guards in their customary attire is stunning.
- Charles Bridge (Karlv most), which spans the Vltava River, is a beloved landmark of

Prague and a pedestrian's paradise. This Gothic bridge offers beautiful views of the city and is decorated with 30 baroque figures.
- Take your time admiring the different statues that line the bridge; each has a unique meaning and tale. The most well-known statue is that of St. John of Nepomuk, whose touch is said to bring luck.
- Street Performers: Enjoy Charles Bridge's vibrant environment as it comes to life with street musicians, artists, and vendors. Take in the colorful energy, listen to live music, and peruse beautiful works.
- Charles Bridge at Sunrise or Sunset: The light at sunrise or sunset gives a warm glow over the city, making for a magnificent experience. These are the periods when the bridge is least congested, allowing you to fully enjoy its magnificence.
- River Views: From the bridge, pause to take in the expansive views of Prague. Admire the Prague Castle, the city's

crimson rooftops, and the gushing Vltava River. It's a beautiful location for taking priceless images.

In addition to being works of art, Prague Castle and Charles Bridge serve as reminders of the city's illustrious past and rich cultural legacy. By visiting these sites, you'll be transported back in time and gain a greater understanding of Prague's splendor and elegance.

The Astronomical Clock and Old Town Square

Every traveler to Prague should include Old Town Square and the Astronomical Clock on their list of must-see sights. Let's explore these fascinating websites:

- Old Town Square (Staromstské námst), in the middle of Prague's historic district, is a hive of activity and a display of beautiful architecture. Here's what to anticipate:
- Tyn Church: Behold the towering Gothic spires of this church, which dominate the skyline of the square. It is a remarkable

architectural marvel due to its complex façade and regal interior.
- Explore the interesting Old Town Hall, which houses the renowned Astronomical Clock. Visit the historical rooms and galleries inside the hall or climb the tower for sweeping views of the city.
- St. Nicholas Church: On the edge of the square, take in the Baroque splendor of St. Nicholas Church. Its magnificent dome and ornate internal embellishments are breathtaking.
- Historical Buildings: Admire the charming facades of the buildings in the square's neighborhood that are painted in soft pastel hues. These buildings, many of which are medieval in origin, provide a window into Prague's lengthy past.
- Cafés & Street entertainers: Take in the vibrant ambiance of the square as street entertainers enthrall the masses with their music and performances. At one of the outside cafés, you may relax with a meal or a cup of coffee while taking in the energetic atmosphere.

- Astronomical Clock (Prask orloj): The Astronomical Clock, a feature of the Old Town Hall and a well-liked Prague attraction, is a remarkable wonder of medieval engineering. What makes it so unique is as follows:
- Hourly Show: The astronomical clock's hourly show is not to be missed. The clock comes to life as the hour strikes, with sculptures of the Apostles emerging from the windows and a parade of moving statues representing various facets of life.
- The astronomical dial, which shows the positions of the sun, moon, zodiac signs, and other celestial information, is a sight to behold. It's an impressive show of astronomy expertise from the Middle Ages.
- Calendar Dial: The calendar dial, which shows the months and seasons, is located beneath the astronomical dial. Numerous Czech holidays and zodiac signs are also depicted.
- Viewing Platform: Climb the Old Town Hall's tower for a close-up look at the

astronomical clock and expansive city views. It's a special vantage point from which to admire Prague's stunning skyline.

Both the Astronomical Clock and the Old Town Square serve as symbols of Prague's illustrious past and exquisite architecture. They provide you with a look into Prague's past and give you a thrilling experience that will make you marvel at Prague's allure. Don't pass up the chance to see these amazing sites while you're here.

Lesser Town and Petn Hill

Lesser Town (Malá Strana) and Petn Hill are two charming Prague neighborhoods that are well worth visiting. Let's examine these lovely locations in more detail:

- Lesser Town (Malá Strana) is a picturesque district with winding lanes, opulent buildings, and a laid-back ambiance that is nestled beneath Prague Castle. What you can find in this historic area is as follows:

- Baroque Architecture: Be amazed by the area's exquisite Baroque architecture. A few of the architectural wonders you'll see include the opulent St. Nicholas Church, the massive Wallenstein Palace, and the beautiful Ernn Palace.
- Visit the well-known Lennon Wall, a vibrant memorial to John Lennon and a sign of harmony and love. Graffiti, poetry, and messages that celebrate creativity and freedom are all over it.
- Kampa Island: Often referred to as the "Venice of Prague," Kampa Island is a gorgeous island that offers breathtaking vistas, riverfront cafes, and art installations, making it the ideal place for a stroll.
- Lesser Town Square: Take a stroll around the quaint Lesser Town Square (Malostranské námst), which features a stunning St. Nicholas Church and lovely façades. The well-known Infant Jesus of Prague monument is also located on the square.
- Views of the Charles Bridge and the lovely Ertovka Canal: Stroll down this

picturesque canal that runs through Lesser Town to take in views of the Charles Bridge from a different angle. This serene location provides a pleasant refuge from the busy masses.

Petn Hill is a green haven that is right across the Vltava River from Lesser Town, where you may get away from the hustle and bustle of the city. What you can do on Petn Hill is as follows:
- Petn Tower: Climb the Petn Tower, a scaled-down counterpart of the Eiffel Tower, for sweeping panoramas over Prague. You are rewarded for your ascent with breathtaking views of the city's roofs, spires, and surroundings.
- Explore the tranquil Petn Gardens, a sizable park studded with attractive walkways, well-kept lawns, and vibrant flowerbeds. The grounds are ideal for a calm picnic in the middle of nature or a stroll.
- Mirror Maze: Have fun at the unique attraction the Mirror Maze, where you can get lost in a labyrinth of warped

reflections. Both children and adults will find it to be lively and enjoyable.
- Find the ruins of the medieval barrier known as the Hunger Wall, which was constructed during a time of hunger. Learn about this building's intriguing history as you stroll over it.
- Petn Funicular: Take the Petn Funicular for a convenient and enjoyable method to ascend the hill. As you make your way to the summit, savor the picturesque trek and take in the expansive vistas.

Lesser Town and Petn Hill both offer a peaceful retreat from the busy city center and an opportunity to take in Prague's scenic beauty and historic charm. Whether you're taking a stroll through the charming alleyways of Lesser Town or taking in the scenery from Petn Hill, these locations provide a singular and unforgettable experience right in the middle of the city.

Cultural Organizations, Museums, and Galleries

Prague has a diverse range of museums, galleries, and cultural organizations that provide intriguing insights into the city's history and culture. Prague is a city rich in culture, history, and artistic expression. Here are some noteworthy ones to investigate:

- The largest museum in the Czech Republic is the National Museum (Národn Muzeum), which is situated at the top of Wenceslas Square. It is home to enormous collections of natural history, archaeology, art, and other subjects. It gives a thorough overview of the nation's scientific and cultural history.

Prague Castle Museums: The Prague Castle complex is home to several museums that highlight various facets of Czech history and culture:

- Explore an excellent collection of European paintings from the 15th to the 18th centuries at the Prague Castle Picture Gallery, which includes pieces by

well-known artists including Titian, Rubens, and Veronese.
- History of Prague Castle's Buildings: Explore the Old Royal Palace, the Basilica of St. George, and the Rosenberg Palace, which are home to several exhibitions and collections, to learn about their fascinating histories.
- The Museum of Communism is a museum that explores life under totalitarian control through multimedia exhibitions, relics, and human accounts. It is situated in the center of Prague.
- DOX Centre for Contemporary Art: DOX is a renowned museum of contemporary art that hosts provocative exhibitions and installations that address modern trends, social challenges, and experimental art. There is a cafe and a bookstore there as well.
- The National Gallery in Prague (Národn Galerie v Praze) has numerous locations throughout the city and has a sizable collection of Czech and foreign artwork from a variety of historical periods and artistic disciplines. The Kinsky Palace,

Sternberg Palace, and the Convent of St. Agnes of Bohemia are important locations.
- The Mucha Museum offers a look at the grace and beauty of the Art Nouveau style through its exhibition of the famous Art Nouveau artist Alphonse Mucha's classic paintings, posters, and decorative art.
- The Jewish Museum in Prague (idovské Muzeum) preserves and shows the rich history and traditions of Prague's Jewish population. It is made up of several locations, including the Jewish Quarter and synagogues. It houses memorials, antiques, and exhibitions.
- The Prague City Gallery, also known as Galerie Hlavnho msta Prahy, exhibits contemporary and modern Czech art in several locations throughout the city. It features up-and-coming regional artists and provides a variety of artistic experiences.
- The Franz Kafka Museum is devoted to the life and works of the eminent author Franz Kafka and explores his literary

legacy, private correspondence, and close ties to Prague.
- The Prague National Theatre, or Národn divadlo, is a cultural center that presents opera, ballet, and theater acts but is not a standard museum or gallery. It serves as both a platform for top-notch artistic productions and a source of pride for the country.

These are only a few of the numerous museums, art galleries, and other cultural establishments Prague has to offer. There are many possibilities to discover and immerse yourself in the city's rich cultural environment, regardless of your interests in history, art, literature, or performing arts.

Nightlife and Dining in Prague

With a variety of gastronomic delights and entertainment alternatives, Prague has a thriving eating and nightlife scene. Here is a sample of the food and entertainment options available in the city:

Dining

Czech Cuisine: Indulge in hearty dishes like goulash, svková (marinated beef with cream sauce), and knedlky (dumplings) from the country's traditional menu. Try some regional favorites like fried cheese and delicious pastries like trdelnk.

International cuisine: Prague is a fusion of diverse tastes. Discover eateries that serve a variety of foods, such as Italian, Asian, Mediterranean, and more. There are several solutions available to accommodate different tastes and nutritional needs.

Prague is no different from the rest of the Czech Republic in that it has a thriving beer culture. To enjoy a range of regional brews, including well-known Czech lagers like Pilsner Urquell and Budvar, visit classic pubs, microbreweries, or beer gardens.

Discover the city's café culture by stopping by quaint coffee shops and cafés. Enjoy a cup of coffee, treat yourself to some delectable pastries, and take in the calm atmosphere while people-watching or reading.

Nightlife

- Bars & Pubs: Prague has a vibrant bar scene with a wide variety of places to spend a night out. You can find a location to fit your preferences, from hip cocktail bars to classic Czech pubs. Try the local liquors like Becherovka and Slivovice if you haven't already.
- Music Clubs: Prague has a flourishing live music scene, with venues playing jazz, rock, electronic, and classical music, among other genres. Enjoy a night of small live performances by artists from across the world and the local community.
- Nightclubs: Dance the night away in one of Prague's clubs, which offer upbeat environments and a variety of music

tastes. Numerous clubs hold weekly themed parties with well-known DJs.
- River Cruises: Take a gorgeous river cruise down the Vltava River for a memorable evening out. As you eat, drink, and listen to live music, take in Prague's lighted sights from a new angle.
- Alternative Venues: Prague boasts a thriving alternative scene, with secret speakeasies, art galleries, and underground clubs. These places provide unusual encounters, live performances, and a window into Prague's underground cultures.
- Safety Advice: When taking in Prague's nightlife, as in any city, it's crucial to use caution and pay attention to your surroundings. To ensure a secure and pleasurable experience, take the required measures.

Prague provides a broad and fascinating choice of dining and nightlife alternatives to suit every taste and mood, whether you like a nice dinner, a laid-back evening at a bar, or an energizing night of dancing.

CHAPTER 4

Learning about Czech Regions

Greetings from the fascinating world of the Czech provinces! Beyond the enchanting city of Prague, there is a rich tapestry of natural features, cultural landmarks, and undiscovered attractions just waiting to be discovered. Each region of the Czech Republic offers a different experience and a chance to delve into the country's rich history and culture, from the scenic countryside and majestic mountains to charming towns and historical landmarks. The Czech regions offer something for everyone, whether you're looking for outdoor activities, want to learn about the local folklore, or just want to enjoy traditional cuisine. Prepare to set off on an adventure of discovery as we reveal the beauty and charm of each location and invite you to explore the hidden tales and treasures that this alluring nation has to offer.

Bohemia

Welcome to Bohemia, a historical region known for its stunning natural scenery, magnificent buildings, and extensive cultural history. Bohemia, which is located in the western region of the Czech Republic, is home to a wealth of activities that will take you back in time and enthrall you with its beauty.

Learn more about Prague, the dynamic capital city, where historic forts, beautiful cathedrals, and quaint cobblestone streets combine with contemporary conveniences and a lively environment. Admire the magnificence of Prague Castle, cross the famous Charles Bridge, and meander through the picturesque Old Town's winding streets. The city is a must-visit destination because of its rich creative and intellectual history as well as its exciting nightlife.

Explore the region outside of Prague to experience Bohemia's spectacular natural splendor. Find more about the luscious Bohemian Forest (umava), a stunning national park that runs along the German border and features lovely hiking routes, serene lakes, and fascinating fauna. Admire the mysterious Bohemian Switzerland (eské vcarsko) rock formations and the striking Adrpach-Teplice Rocks sandstone pillars. These scenic attractions offer a peaceful getaway from the city and a chance to re-establish contact with nature.

By visiting historic cities and UNESCO World Heritage Sites, you may delve into the fascinating history of Bohemia. Explore the picturesque riverfront setting and the fairytale castle of the medieval village of Esk Krumlov. Explore the quaint town of Kutná Hora, which is renowned for the majestic Gothic Cathedral of St. Barbara and the stunning Bone Church (Sedlec Ossuary). Every town has a distinct history to share that provides a window into the past of the area.

Experience the rich culture and customs of Bohemia while indulging in hearty Czech food and famous Czech beer. While savoring the warm friendliness of the people, sample traditional fare like svková (marinated beef with cream sauce) and trdelnk (a sweet pastry). Bohemia cordially welcomes you to set out on a discovery adventure where nature, history, and culture converge to produce a memorable experience. Allow Bohemia to captivate your heart and leave you with lifelong memories, from the energetic city of Prague to the serene countryside.

Český Krumlov

Welcome to Český Krumlov, a charming village that will take you back in time that is tucked away in the middle of Bohemia. Beautiful medieval architecture that has been kept The Czech Republic's Český Krumlov is a real treasure that enchants travelers from all over the world with its cobblestone streets and meandering river. Discover the UNESCO World Heritage Site's old core and get lost in its labyrinth of winding lanes and quaint squares. The stately castle in "Český" Krumlov, one of the biggest in Central Europe, serves as the town's focal point. Step inside and take in the splendor of the Renaissance and Baroque architectural styles as you meander around the courtyards, gardens, and elaborate interiors. Enjoy the stunning views of the castle reflected in the water as you meander down the Vltava River, the town's lifeblood. Take a leisurely boat trip or just unwind at one of the riverfront cafés while taking in the peace and beauty of the area.

The Egon Schiele Art Centrum, which displays the creations of this well-known Austrian painter who formerly resided in Esk Krumlov, will please art enthusiasts. Immerse yourself in Schiele's expressive works to learn more about his life and development as an artist.

Attend a show in the baroque-style Esk Krumlov Castle Theater for a distinctive cultural encounter. This elegant venue for a night of entertainment continues to produce operas, ballets and plays in its historic theater that dates back to the 17th century.
Experience the flavors of "esk" Krumlov by trying out typical Czech fare at nearby eateries and pubs. Savor the region's diverse culinary traditions by serving your meal with a glass of superb Czech beer or delectable Moravian wine.

Explore the picturesque scenery that surrounds Esk Krumlov outside of the town's center. Visit the breathtaking Romberk Castle, go on a trek through the nearby Bohemian Forest, or engage in outdoor pursuits like rafting or cycling along the beautiful pathways.

Krumlov is a town that mixes history, art, stunning natural scenery, and friendly people with ease. It's charming ambiance and medieval charm will take you to another time, leaving you with lifelong memories. Learn about the mystique of "esk" Krumlov and allow its enduring attraction to seduce you.

Karlovy Vary

Welcome to Karlovy Vary, a charming spa city tucked away in one of Bohemia's lush valleys. Karlovy Vary is a refreshing vacation that has drawn tourists seeking wellness and leisure for generations. It is well-known for its natural hot springs, gorgeous architecture, and peaceful ambiance. The magnificent colonnades flanking the Teplá River will welcome you as you arrive; each is embellished with elaborate pavilions where mineral-rich thermal springs flow. Enjoy the therapeutic benefits of drinking healing waters from vintage spa cups, which are thought to improve digestion and general health.

Explore the lovely city center, which is dotted with impressive structures that display exquisite architecture from many eras. Look at the impressive colonnade facades, such as those of the Market Colonnade and the Mill Colonnade, which are not only architectural wonders but also home to a variety of stores, cafes, and spa facilities. Experience the spa lifestyle by indulging in a variety of wellness services. Karlovy Vary provides a wide range of choices to soothe your body and soul, including opulent spa rituals, therapeutic massages, and healing baths. Don't pass up the chance to partake in the local practice known as "kolonáda," which involves having warm

mineral water poured over your body to promote relaxation and renewal.
Explore the quaint streets that are lined with chic boutiques, independent stores, and inviting cafes. Be sure to peruse the local shops for one-of-a-kind porcelain keepsakes to bring home since Karlovy Vary is also renowned for its fine porcelain.

Try the town's specialty, Karlovarské oplatky, a delicate wafer cookie that comes in a variety of flavors, to get a taste of the town's gastronomic delights. Enjoy hearty delicacies like svková and mouthwatering dumplings at cozy restaurants as well as a sip of the regional Becherovka liqueur, which is distinguished by its herbal and somewhat bitter flavor. Explore the surrounding natural splendor outside of the town. Visit the adjacent Moser Glassworks to see the fine artistry of Bohemian crystal glass or go on a picturesque trek through the forested hills and verdant woodlands.
Karlovy Vary offers a getaway for rest, renewal, and a dash of luxury with its tranquil ambiance, healing waters, and classic elegance. Experience the therapeutic benefits of the area's hot

springs, acquaint yourself with the town's illustrious spa customs, and allow the beauty of Karlovy Vary to engulf you in a sense of calm and well-being.

Plzeň

Welcome to Plzeň a thriving city in western Bohemia with a major role in the beer industry. Plze, the birthplace of the well-known Pilsner beer, draws both beer connoisseurs and history buffs with its rich brewing past, alluring architecture, and dynamic environment.

Start your trip at the beautiful Republic Square (námst Republiky) in the center of the city. This area is home to the beautiful St. Bartholomew's Cathedral in Gothic architecture, which commands the skyline with its high spire. Enter to see the beautiful interior and finely crafted stained glass windows, which are evidence of the city's historical importance.

For beer connoisseurs, a trip to the Pilsner Urquell Brewery is essential. Take a tour with a guide to learn about the brewing process, see how the renowned Pilsner beer is made, and even get a taste straight from the oak barrels.

Learn about the brewery's remarkable past, which begins in 1842 when it produced the first golden Pilsner beer, transforming the global beer market.

Visit the Pilsen Beer Museum in the old city basements if you want to learn more about the world of beer. Explore engaging exhibitions and displays that tell the tale of Plze's brewing heritage to better understand the city's beer culture. Admire the beautiful architecture that captures several historical eras as you stroll around Plze's quaint streets. One of the biggest Jewish synagogues in Europe, The Great Synagogue, combines Moorish and Art Nouveau design elements. Take a stroll down Republic Street (Republikánská ulice) and enjoy the eye-catching storefronts and bright facades.

The Techmania Science Center is a hands-on museum in Plzen where visitors of all ages can conduct experiments, learn about science and technology, and investigate a variety of scientific phenomena.

Visit Plzen during the yearly Pilsner Fest, a vibrant festival of beer, music, and Czech culture, to become fully immersed in local customs. Enjoy live entertainment, regional cuisine, and, of course, a broad variety of delectable brews.

Plzen provides an unforgettable tour that honors the craft of brewing and the vivacious Czech friendliness.

Moravia

Welcome to Moravia, the Czech Republic's easternmost area, where you'll find picturesque cities, verdant countryside, and rich cultural history. Moravia invites you to experience its stunning natural surroundings, savor its world-class wines, and become engrossed in its vibrant traditions. It is known for its rolling hills, attractive vineyards, and kind hospitality.

Learn about the fascinating capital of the region, Brno, which skillfully combines old-world charm with contemporary vitality. Discover the fascinating history of the hilltop castle, Pilberk, which served as a fortification, a prison, and a museum. Explore the Old Town's vibrant streets while seeing the Gothic-style St. Peter and Paul Cathedral and taking in the lively ambiance of Freedom Square (námst Svobody).

A trip to Moravia would be incomplete without visiting the region's vineyards and wine cellars because the country is known for producing fine wines. Join a wine tour through the South Moravian Wine Region to try some of the region's world-renowned wines, including Grüner Veltliner, Riesling, and Veltlnské zelené. Visit family-run wineries, take a stroll through the vineyards, and speak with enthusiastic neighborhood vintners to learn more about the winemaking process.

Escape to the captivating Lednice-Valtice Cultural Landscape, a 200 square-kilometer area designated as a UNESCO World Heritage Site. Admire the magnificent Lednice and Valtice Castles, which are encircled by well-kept gardens, tranquil lakes, and charming follies. Relax and take in the lovely beauty of this fairytale-like setting, take a leisurely boat ride on the decorative ponds, or just take it all in.

Visit the lovely town of Olomouc to become fully immersed in the customs and folklore of the Moravians. Observe its magnificent Baroque Holy Trinity Column, which is listed by UNESCO.

stroll around the charming Upper Square (Horn námst), which is surrounded by vibrant buildings and bustling cafés. Try Olomouc's well-known "tvarky," a strong cheese with a peculiar flavor that has become a regional delicacy.

The Moravian Karst, a magnificent karst terrain with deep caverns, enigmatic caves, and lush forests, is a haven for nature lovers. Discover the expansive network of caves in the Punkva region, including the renowned Macocha Abyss, where you may take a boat ride on an underground river and gaze in awe at the mesmerizing rock formations.

Folk customs, holidays, and craftsmanship all serve to highlight Moravia's illustrious cultural past. Moravia provides a glimpse into its rich heritage with vivid traditional costumes, lively folk dances, and delicate hand-painted pottery in the town of Modrá.

You are invited to travel to Moravia to experience its stunning scenery, world-class wines, and centuries-old customs. Enjoy the warm hospitality of the area, revel in its delectable cuisine, and allow the alluring spirit of Moravia to seduce you.

Brno

Welcome to Brno, Moravia's vibrant and culturally significant capital city. Located in the center of the area, Brno charms and inspires visitors with its alluring fusion of history, modernity, and a lively atmosphere.

Start your trip at the renowned Pilberk Castle in the center of the city. This 13th-century stronghold turned museum towers above Brno and provides panoramic views of the city and

exhibits works that explore its intriguing past. Discover the stories of the castle's former prisoners while exploring the museum's exhibits and the castle's underground tunnels.
Explore the Old Town's lovely alleyways where Baroque and medieval styles of architecture mix peacefully. Admire the St. Peter and Paul Cathedral, a notable structure that dominates the skyline of the city. Visit Freedom Square (námst Svobody), a bustling center with the classic Baroque Parnas Fountain and a variety of stores, cafes, and restaurants, to experience its vibrant atmosphere.
With its abundance of theaters, galleries, and museums, Brno is a city rich in culture and innovation. Explore the intriguing displays at the Moravian Museum, which highlights the area's rich history, archaeology, and natural sciences, or pay a visit to the Moravian Gallery, which is home to a sizable collection of modern and contemporary art. Visit the Janáek Theatre,

renowned for its superb opera and ballet shows, or the Brno National Theatre to take in the dynamic cultural scene.

Try traditional Moravian cuisine in the crowded markets for a sample of the regional delicacies. Try delectable regional specialties like svková, a meal of marinated beef with a creamy sauce, and savor regional wines, especially the famed Moravian white wines that flourish in the nearby vineyards.

People who love nature will value Brno's accessibility to stunning natural areas. Explore the adjacent Moravian Karst's picturesque grandeur, which includes spectacular caves and underground rivers. Join a tour guide to explore the fascinating Macocha Abyss and Punkva Caves, where you can explore underground waterways and take in the stunning stalactite formations.

The Moravian Autumn music festival, which honors both traditional and contemporary music, and the Ignis Brunensis fireworks competition are just two of the exciting events and festivals that take place every year in Brno.

Brno offers a distinctive and genuine experience in the center of Moravia with its enthralling history, rich culture, and active atmosphere. Take in the charm of the city, give in to its creative spirit, and let Brno's energetic character leave a lasting impression on your voyage.

Olomouc

Hello and welcome to Olomouc, a jewel tucked away in Moravia. Olomouc offers a fascinating voyage through centuries of tradition and artistic legacy with its rich history, breathtaking architecture, and thriving cultural scene.

Start your trip at the Holy Trinity Column in the Upper Square (Horn námst), a spectacular Baroque structure that is on the UNESCO World Heritage List. Admire the fine intricacies of this masterwork, which honors the plague victims and displays the exceptional skill of the time.

Explore the Old Town of Olomouc's lovely squares and picture-perfect streets to find historical sites. Explore the Astronomical Clock's splendor and observe how it comes to life with its exquisite figurines and astronomical displays. It is situated on the Town Hall's façade.

Visit the magnificent St. Wenceslas Cathedral, which represents the spiritual importance of Olomouc. Enter to behold its elaborate chapels, Gothic architecture, and a magnificent organ. For sweeping vistas of the city and a look at its rich history, climb the tower.

A famous university is also located in Olomouc, giving the city a lively and youthful vibe. Explore the busy student district, which is home to cafes, bookshops, and cultural institutions, and take a stroll across the university campus to take in the intellectual atmosphere.

The Archdiocesan Museum, housed in the Krom Archbishops' Palace, will appeal to art lovers. Learn about the impressive gardens, historical treasures, and rich collection of religious art that have made this place a UNESCO World Heritage Site.

Enjoy Olomouc's delectable local cuisine, which is renowned for its world-class cheese. Try the peculiar Olomouc tvarky, a strong, crumbly cheese that has become a trademark of the area. Enjoy traditional Czech cuisine in quaint eateries while sipping a glass of Moravian wine or locally brewed beer.

Attend one of the many festivals, concerts, or plays in Olomouc to fully experience the city's rich cultural scene. There is always something captivating going on in Olomouc, from the brilliant Flora Olomouc flower display to the vibrant music events that bring the city to life.

Step outside the city's center to discover the breathtaking natural surroundings. Visit the adjacent Litovel Brewery to discover more about the brewing process and to try some of their well-known brews. Discover the charming Bouzov Castle, which is set on a hilltop and will transport you to a land of fairies and knights.

Olomouc cordially invites you to explore its enticing attractions, savor its fascinating past, and take in its vivacious culture. Explore its architectural beauty, relish its culinary treats, and let the welcoming atmosphere leave a lasting effect on your trip through Moravia.

Mikulov

Hello and welcome to Mikulov, a quaint hamlet tucked away in the South Moravian Wine Region. Mikulov welcomes you to revel in its wine culture, delve into its rich past, and acquaint yourself with its stunning landscapes. It is surrounded by rolling vineyards, studded with ancient sites, and possessing breathtaking natural beauty.

Start your journey in the town center, where the majestic Mikulov Castle dominates. This magnificent Baroque castle towers over the town and provides breathtaking all-encompassing views of the surrounding landscape. Learn about the fascinating history of the noble families that formerly lived here by exploring its opulent rooms and the castle museum.

Explore the Old Town of Mikulov's lovely streets, which are lined with vibrant architecture, inviting squares, and modest cafes. Admire the town hall's and Holy Hill's architectural splendor, which contains the Holy Trinity Chapel and the Church of St. Sebastian.

Take a minute to unwind and taste exquisite wines in one of the little wine cellars.

local wines and discover the traditions of winemaking that have been passed down for many years.

The various vineyards and wineries that surround Mikulov will excite wine lovers. Visit family-run wineries, go on a guided tour of the vineyards, and sample some of the world-famous Moravian white wines including Riesling, Grüner Veltliner, and Veltlnské zelené. Don't pass up the chance to take part in one of Mikulov's yearly wine festivals, where you can enjoy the harvest and soak up the vibrant atmosphere of the city's wine culture.

The Pálava Landscape Protected Area is a special natural reserve around Mikulov that is a haven for nature lovers. Explore the mysterious limestone formations, embark on a hiking or cycling journey along the beautiful pathways, and take in the breathtaking views from the summit of the Pálava Hills. On the shores of the Nové Mlny reservoirs, explore the lovely village of Pavlov. Participate in water sports or just unwind on the serene beaches.

Visit the Jewish Quarter to fully appreciate Mikulov's rich history and cultural heritage. Discover one of the biggest Jewish cemeteries in Central Europe, Mikulov, and travel to the synagogue, which is now a museum highlighting the heritage and customs of the neighborhood's Jewish population.

Mikulov cordially invites you to sample its wine, discover its historical sites, and take in its breathtaking scenery. The greatest of South Moravia's wine area is celebrated in Mikulov, a thrilling and unforgettable experience for everyone who enjoys wine, history, or the outdoors.

Additional Important Areas

Mountains of Beskydy

Welcome to the Beskydy Mountains, a breathtaking mountain chain that straddles Poland, Slovakia, and the Czech Republic. With its untainted environment, lovely scenery, and

The Beskydy Mountains are a paradise for outdoor enthusiasts and nature lovers with their lovely mountain communities.

Explore the lush forests on foot to find a network of defined trails that will take you to beautiful vistas and undiscovered waterfalls. The Beskydy Mountains become a beautiful wonderland in the winter and welcome visitors to engage in winter sports such as skiing and snowboarding.

Don't pass up the chance to see the Wallachian Open-Air Museum, which is located in the quaint village of Ronov pod Radhotm. This one-of-a-kind museum allows visitors to travel back in time and enjoy the rich heritage of the area by showcasing the traditional Wallachian architecture, folk culture, and way of life.

Bohemia North

Welcome to North Bohemia, an area known for its stunning architecture, varied landscapes, and long history. North Bohemia has much to offer any traveler, from the sandstone cliffs of the Bohemian Switzerland National Park to the ancient spa town of Karlovy Vary.

Admire the extraordinary rock formations of Bohemian Switzerland, which resemble a fantastical environment. Explore the park's captivating gorges, canyons, and waterfalls, or go on a climb to the Pravická Gate, the biggest natural sandstone arch in Europe.

Visit the attractive riverbank promenade and restored old center of Litomice, a picturesque town. Take a stroll around the vibrant streets, observe St. Stephen's Cathedral's Gothic design, and take in the tranquil ambiance of this hidden jewel.

Get lost in Karlovy Vary's spa culture for a taste of luxury and relaxation. Enjoy the therapeutic benefits of the mineral-rich thermal springs, stroll along the graceful colonnades, and try the world-famous Karlovy Vary wafers and conventional herbal liquor.

North Bohemia is also the location of a bevy of architectural wonders, such as the magnificent Prague Castle, the famous Charles Bridge, and the historic town of Kutná Hora with its breathtaking Sedlec Ossuary (Bone Church), which is inscribed on the UNESCO World Heritage List.

With its stunning natural scenery, rich cultural past, and magnificent architecture, North Bohemia enchants tourists and offers them an unforgettable historical tour and enthralling sceneries.

CHAPTER 5
Outdoor Activities and Natural Wonders

Welcome to the Czech Republic, a beautiful natural setting with a wealth of outdoor recreation opportunities. The Czech Republic provides a wide range of chances for nature enthusiasts and those looking for adventure, from rolling hills and scenic valleys to breathtaking mountains and peaceful lakes.

Immerse yourself in the unspoiled grandeur of the Bohemian Switzerland National Park, where towering sandstone cliffs, deep gorges, and enigmatic forests produce a wonderfully beautiful ambiance. Explore the area on foot to find secret paths, stunning vistas, and unusual rock formations, including the famous Pravická Gate, the biggest natural sandstone arch in Europe.

The Czech Republic provides exhilarating outdoor excursions for thrill seekers. The towering cliffs of Adrspach-Teplice Rocks, a maze of sandstone formations that will inspire and challenge you, are a great place to practice rock climbing. A different option is to go to the Sumava National Park, where you may explore its extensive network of hiking and cycling routes, go kayaking along beautiful rivers, or even go wildlife watching.

Get ready to set off on a trip of exploration and adventure in this breathtaking land by lacing up your hiking boots, grabbing your camera, and getting ready.

Bohemian Paradise

You are cordially invited to Bohemian Paradise, a beautiful locale tucked away in the center of the Czech Republic. Bohemian Paradise is a haven for nature lovers and outdoor adventurers, known for its unusual rock formations, lush forests, and serene landscape.

The spectacular sandstone rock formations that characterize this beautiful region will astound you. Explore Trosky, a famous rock town where two castle tower ruins from the medieval era rise atop striking rock pillars like something from a fairy tale. Discover the bizarre beauty of Prachov Rocks, a labyrinth of soaring sandstone pillars and obscure corridors that is ideal for trekking, climbing, and finding secret perspectives.

The different ecosystems of Bohemian Paradise will provide comfort to those who appreciate nature. Set out on beautiful hiking paths that meander through lovely valleys, meadows covered with wildflowers, and tranquil forests alive with the sounds of birds. View the expansive surroundings from the picturesque Hrubá Skála Castle, built on a sandstone ridge.

Take a hot air balloon ride or go paragliding for a distinctive view of the area. Take in the breathtaking views that Bohemian Paradise has to offer as you soar above the spectacular rock formations, forests, and rolling landscapes.

The tiny village of Ji'n, frequently referred to as the "Gateway to Bohemian Paradise," exudes a timeless charm with its well-preserved historic center, vibrant facades, and quaint cobblestone streets. Visit the charming Valdtejn Castle, stroll through the tranquil Wallenstein Gardens, and savor authentic Czech fare at nearby eateries.

Numerous bicycle tracks can be found in Bohemian Paradise, inviting you to tour the area on two wheels. Bike across the countryside, past quaint towns, gurgling rivers, and lush meadows. To enjoy a picnic outdoors or to explore nearby farms and experience delectable local fare, take a break along the road.

Bohemian Paradise offers a one-of-a-kind and amazing experience, whether you're looking for adventure, peace, or just a connection with nature. This natural playground will leave you in amazement and yearning to return to its splendor repeatedly, from the captivating rock formations to the tranquil landscapes.

Šumava National Park

Hello and welcome to Šumava National Park, a little-known treasure tucked away in the southwest of the Czech Republic. This stunning national park, which stretches across the Umava Mountains and borders Germany and Austria, is a paradise for nature lovers, outdoor enthusiasts, and anyone looking for peace in untainted settings.

Get ready to be mesmerized by the park's various ecosystems, which include luxuriant spruce and fir tree forests, meandering rivers, tranquil lakes, and enormous peat bogs. Put on your hiking boots and explore the network of clearly marked paths that meander through the park. These routes will take you to stunning vistas, remote waterfalls, and undiscovered delights.

Numerous animals can be found at Umava National Park, including the elusive lynx, wolves, and golden eagles. As you set out on a voyage of animal observation, keep an eye out and get your camera ready. Birdwatchers will be enthralled by the park's different ecosystems, which are home to a wide variety of bird species.

The scenic Lake Lipno, the biggest reservoir in the Czech Republic, is one of the park's features. Enjoy a day of leisurely exploration of the lake's shoreline while engaging in water sports like fishing, kayaking, or paddleboarding. The tranquil backdrop of the lake offers the ideal environment for unwinding and re-establishing contact with nature.

Sumava National Park changes into a winter paradise in the winter and offers a variety of activities for snow lovers. Put on your skis or snowshoes and tackle the trails, or go cross-country skiing or snowboarding in the park's icy terrain. A magnificent ambiance is created by the park's pure winter beauty and serene tranquility.

Visit the charming towns dotted around Sumava National Park as you explore it. Immerse yourself in the rich stories and customs that have formed this region for generations, experience traditional Czech food, and get a taste of the local warmth and culture.

The tranquility of untainted nature is offered to you by Sumava National Park as a means of escaping the stress of daily life. Umava National Park guarantees a memorable experience that will leave you with long-lasting memories of this unspoiled environment, whether you're seeking adventure, solitude, or a closer connection with the natural world.

National Park of Krkonoše

The Czech Republic's northern Krkonoše National Park is a magnificent natural treasure just waiting to be discovered. This stunning national park is home to the Krkonoe Mountains and is a haven for hikers, mountaineers, and environment lovers.
Krkonoe National Park's untamed beauty is quite breathtaking. The park offers a breathtaking view of the alpine terrain with its towering peaks, deep valleys, and tumbling waterfalls. Snka, the highest peak in the Czech

Republic, is located in the center of the park. Take an exhilarating walk to the summit, where you'll be rewarded with expansive views across the lovely valleys and rolling hills below. Krkonose National Park is home to stunning mountains as well as a thriving ecosystem. The park is home to numerous endangered plant and animal species, including the chamois, a type of mountain goat. Explore the park's natural forests, meandering rivers, and serene lakes at your own pace, and keep an eye out for wildlife encounters. Explore the vast network of hiking paths in the park, which are suitable for hikers of all skill levels. There is a trail for everyone, whether you're an experienced hiker searching for a strenuous ascent or a casual walker looking for a picturesque stroll. You'll pass through stunning terrain along the way.

Krkonose National Park changes into a snowy wonderland throughout the colder months. With fantastic options for skiing, snowboarding, and cross-country skiing, the area is a sanctuary for fans of winter sports. Go skiing at well-known ski areas like Pindlerv

Mln, Harrachov, or Pec pod Snkou to feel the rush of gliding down fluffy slopes.

Take some time to consider the region's cultural and historical significance while you tour Krkonose National Park. Visit authentic mountain communities to experience local culture firsthand, sample authentic cuisine, and gain insight into the rich folklore that has defined this region for centuries.

You are invited to explore the beauties of Krkonose National Park's mighty mountains and pristine alpine sceneries. This national park offers an extraordinary tour that will leave you with enduring memories of its spectacular beauty, whether you're seeking adventure, peace, or a closer connection with nature.

Adršpach-Teplice Rocks

The northeastern region of the Czech Republic is home to the Adrspach-Teplice Rocks, which allow you to enter a spellbinding natural wonder. With its towering sandstone pillars, secret corridors, and breathtaking scenery, this unusual rock formation complex enchants tourists and delivers a bizarre and engaging experience.

As soon as you step foot inside the Adrspach-Teplice Rocks, you'll be surrounded by a bizarre universe of formations and shapes. This natural labyrinth of sandstone pillars, which is the consequence of millions of years of erosion, exhibits nature's amazing artistic talent. Get ready to be in wonder as you observe the striking cliffs, spire-like structures that seem to defy gravity, and exquisite rock formations.

Discover the network of pathways that meander through this spectacular environment and take you to secret caverns just waiting to be found. Follow the trail as it meanders through confined gorges, enigmatic tunnels, and spectacular vistas, each providing a fresh outlook on the bizarre beauty of the rocks.

Deeper within the Adrspach-Teplice Rocks, you'll find peaceful lakes tucked amid the rock formations that reflect the cliffs around them and create a tranquil ambiance. Take a leisurely boat ride on one of the lakes and let the serenity of this natural haven wash over you.

The magnificent sandstone formations provide limitless inspiration for photographers. Capture the rich textures, vibrant colors, and light-and-shadow play that embellish these natural sculptures. Every turn unveils a fresh composition, beckoning you to let your imagination run wild.

The Adrspach-Teplice Rocks have also been portrayed in several motion pictures, enhancing their fascination and attractiveness in the movies. You can come upon sights that are reminiscent of a fairy tale or an epic journey as you explore the rocks.

Whether you're a fan of the great outdoors, a lover of nature, or just someone looking for a singular and mind-blowing experience, this remarkable natural wonder will live long in your memory.

Trails for biking and hiking

The Czech Republic has a bevy of cycling and hiking paths that wind across its varied landscapes, making it a haven for outdoor enthusiasts. There is something for everyone to appreciate, from gently sloping hills and picturesque valleys to deep woods and stunning mountains.

The vast network of bike paths that traverse the nation will please cyclists. The Czech Republic has a route for everyone, whether you're an experienced mountain biker looking for heart-pounding descents or a casual rider wanting to see quaint villages and the countryside. Ride your bike through attractive wine areas, alongside charming rivers, or across tough mountain terrain while you slowly take in the beauty of your surroundings.

The country's Greenways trail, which extends from Prague to Vienna, is one of the most well-liked bicycle routes. This well-marked trail offers a combination of cultural and environmental treasures along the way as it leads you past charming cities, UNESCO-listed locations, and idyllic countryside. Another popular route is the Elbe River Cycle Route, which passes through beautiful river scenery, storied cities, and magnificent castles.

The Czech Republic has a vast network of well-maintained hiking paths that are suitable for hikers of all skill levels. Set off on a journey through pristine national parks, picturesque mountain ranges, and peaceful countryside by lacing on your hiking boots. As you immerse yourself in nature's beauty, find secret waterfalls, sweeping vistas, and winding woodland paths.

A hiker's delight, Bohemian Switzerland National Park is situated close to the German border. A maze of trails winds through the park's sandstone rock formations, verdant forests, and narrow valleys. Hike to stunning viewpoints that offer panoramic views of the surrounding landscapes while admiring the legendary Pravická Gate, the largest natural sandstone arch in all of Europe.

Another shelter for hikers is the scenic Sumava National Park in the southwest of the nation. Investigate its varied habitats, which include untouched forests, peaceful lakes, and rolling hills. Explore the stunning Ertovo Jezero (Devil's Lake) or go on the strenuous climb to the top of Snka, the highest peak.

The cycling and hiking paths in the Czech Republic will take you to spectacular natural wonders, undiscovered treasures, and amazing experiences whether you decide to travel the country on two wheels or foot. Pack your bags, embrace your sense of adventure, and savor the natural beauty of this stunning nation.

Winter activities and water sports

Adventurers and outdoor enthusiasts can enjoy a variety of water sports and winter activities throughout the entire year in the Czech Republic. There are plenty of thrills in this varied nation, from heart-pounding winter sports to exhilarating sea excursions.

On the nation's lakes, rivers, and reservoirs, water sports enthusiasts can indulge in a range of activities during the warmer months. Popular options include kayaking and canoeing, which let you go through picturesque waterways, discover secret coves, and enjoy the scenic beauty of the surroundings. Prague's Vltava River provides a great environment for a leisurely paddle, and the Lipno Reservoir offers plenty of sailing and windsurfing opportunities. Try your hand at white-water rafting or hydrospeeding if you want a more exhilarating experience. You can put your talents to the test by navigating the Elbe River's stormy waters or the Ertovka River's rapids. Your heart will race as you partake in these exhilarating water activities, which will offer an unforgettable adventure.

The Czech Republic becomes a winter wonderland as winter coats the nation in a sparkling layer of snow. The region's world-class ski resorts and cross-country skiing paths are available to winter sports lovers. With well-maintained slopes accommodating skiers and snowboarders of all abilities, the Jizera Mountains and Krkonoe Mountains provide some of the best skiing options in the nation.

Put on a pair of snowshoes and experience the pristine winter landscapes at a leisurely pace. Take the routes that lead up to beautiful vistas, past open fields, and through forests covered in snow. Snowshoeing enables you to take in the quiet of nature and take in the splendor of the winter landscape.

Another popular winter pastime in the Czech Republic is ice skating. During the colder months, a lot of towns and cities construct outdoor ice rinks, providing an enjoyable and joyful experience for people of all ages. Navigate the ice with finesse while taking in the allure of winter's surroundings.

The Czech Republic offers a variety of adventurous activities, whether you enjoy the thrill of water sports or the rush of winter sports. So embrace the delights that each season has to offer by jumping into the water or cutting through the snow.

CHAPTER 6

Czech food and traditional treats

Welcoming you to the robust flavors, rich traditions, and gastronomic delights of the world of Czech cuisine. The Czech Republic offers a wide and flavorful culinary experience that will tickle your taste buds and leave you wanting more, from savory meat meals to delightful desserts.

Czechs have a deep-seated affection for homey comfort foods. Enjoy the traditional svková dish, which consists of delicious beef that has been marinated, topped with a creamy sauce, and fluffy dumplings. Enjoy the flavor of goulash, a robust meat stew flavored with paprika and other spices. Don't forget to sample the national cuisine of the Czech Republic, vepo-knedlo-zelo, which consists of tender roast pork served with dumplings and sauerkraut.

Experience the charm of Czech food, where wholesome warmth combines with classic flavors. Each taste will take you further into the heart of Czech culinary traditions, whether you're eating at a quaint neighborhood tavern, a family-run restaurant, or a bustling food market. So go on a culinary tour and enjoy the special flavors of Czech food and its historical delicacies

Customary Czech Food

The robust, delicious meals that characterize Czech cuisine are a reflection of the nation's extensive culinary history. Here are some typical Czech foods that will tickle your taste buds, from savory meats to hearty dumplings and sweet pastries:

- Svková: This traditional Czech cuisine is a slow-cooked beef sirloin that has been marinated, and it is served with a creamy sauce that is produced from root vegetables, spices, and a touch of lemon. It is customarily served with light bread dumplings (knedlky) and a dollop of tart cranberry sauce on top.

- Vepřo-knedlo-zelo: which combines sauerkraut (zel), bread dumplings, and roast pork (vepová peen), is regarded as the national dish of the Czech Republic. Usually, caraway seeds, garlic, and other savory spices are used to season the tender roasted pork.
- Guláš: Tender beef or pork is cooked gently in a rich sauce that is seasoned with paprika, onions, and other spices to create this tasty meat stew known as goulash. It frequently comes with steamed rice or bread dumplings.
- The ingredients for bramboráky, a type of classic potato pancake popular in the Czech Republic, are grated potatoes, eggs, flour, and other flavors including garlic and marjoram. They create a delightful and gratifying snack or side dish when fried till golden and crispy.
- Smažený sýr: A cheese dish deep-fried, is a well-known street food in the Czech Republic. A piece of Hermelin or Edam cheese is breaded and deep-fried till crisp and golden. It usually comes with fries or a side of salad and tartar sauce.

- Trdelnik: A traditional dessert from the Czech Republic, trdelnik is a cylindrical pastry formed from rolled dough that is wound around a metal or wooden rod, grilled, and dusted with sugar and almonds. It can be filled with ice cream, Nutella, or other sweet ingredients and is frequently eaten warm.
- Koláče: these are tiny, sweet snacks that are typically packed with fruit, poppy seeds, or sweet cheese. The fillings vary based on the location and the individual's preferences, and the dough is soft and slightly sweet.

These are only a few of the mouthwatering traditional Czech meals that highlight the nation's rich culinary heritage. Czech food offers a variety of flavors and textures that will leave you wanting more, whether you enjoy meat, dumplings, or sweets. Enjoy the rich traditions of this exceptional culinary heritage as you experience the culinary delights of Czech cuisine.

Well-known Czech brews and beers

The Czech Republic is well-known throughout the world for its outstanding beers and brewing culture. Czech beers are renowned for their quality, flavor, and devotion to time-honored brewing traditions. The nation has a long history of producing beer. The following are some well-known Czech brews and breweries that you ought to be aware of:

- Pilsner Urquell maintains a distinct place in Czech brewing history as one of the most well-known beers in the country. The Pilsner style, known for its golden hue, freshness, and well-balanced hop bitterness, was created in the city of Plze in 1842 and was first brewed there. The beer Pilsner Urquell is still a favorite both in the Czech Republic and abroad.
- Budweiser Budvar: Another well-known Czech beer, Budweiser Budvar hails from the city of eské Budjovice. It is renowned for its smoothness, full-bodied flavor, and distinct hop flavor. Budweiser

Budvar is a prime example of Czech brewing heritage, having been brewed with traditional techniques and locally available ingredients.
- One of the most renowned breweries in Prague is Staropramen, which was established in 1869. A variety of beers are made there, including the well-known Staropramen Lager, which is distinguished by a harmonious balance of malt sweetness and hop bitterness. The brewery also provides additional varieties, such as dark lagers and wheat beers, giving beer fans a wide range of options.
- One of the oldest breweries in the Czech Republic is Krušovice whose history dates back to the 16th century. The ancient techniques and premium ingredients used in the brewing of Kruovice beers, which are renowned for their outstanding lagers, produce a smooth and tasty drinking experience.
- Bernard: The Humpolec-based Bernard Brewery takes pride in its dedication to producing premium, unpasteurized, and

unfiltered beers. Bernard beers, which range from basic lagers to specialty brews, are renowned for their robust flavors, distinctive fragrances, and devotion to traditional brewing methods.
- Kocour: Known for its inventive and artistic brewing methods, Kocour Brewery is a pioneer in the Czech craft beer market. It caters to consumers looking for novel and intriguing beer experiences by offering a wide variety of distinctive and experimental beers, frequently incorporating unusual ingredients and flavors.

These are only a few of the numerous exceptional Czech beers and breweries that have made their mark on the brewing industry. The Czech Republic has a diverse beer culture that appeals to all tastes, whether you want a traditional Pilsner, a deep dark lager, or an experimental craft brew. So raise a glass, enjoy the tastes, and toast to the superior brewing of the Czech Republic. (Cheers!)

Wine Region Areas and Tasting Opportunities

Despite being known for its beer culture, the Czech Republic also has beautiful wine areas and a growing wine industry. The nation provides wine connoisseurs with the chance to tour its vineyards and has excellent tasting experiences due to its long history of winemaking and distinctive grape varietals. Here are some well-known wine-producing areas and what to expect when tasting Czech wine:

- The Moravian: The stronghold of Czech winemaking is the region of Moravia, which is situated in the southeast of the nation. It is renowned for its picturesque wine villages, undulating vineyard-covered landscapes, and a wide variety of wine varieties. With grapes like Grüner Veltliner, Welschriesling, Riesling, Sauvignon Blanc, Pinot Noir, and Saint Laurent, Moravia produces a variety of white, red, and rosé wines. With wine cellars, vineyard tours, and tastings available, the villages of Mikulov,

Znojmo, and Valtice are well-liked vacation spots for wine enthusiasts.
- South Moravia: South Moravia stands out as the main wine-producing area within the Moravian region. This subregion has an excellent climate and rich soil that are perfect for growing grapes. Visitors can tour the picturesque wine towns of Velké Pavlovice, Valtice, and Znojmo and partake in wine tastings at nearby wineries and cellars. For lovers of wine, Mikulov, with its castle and vineyards, is a must-visit location.
- Bohemia: While Moravia garners much of the attention for Czech winemaking, the western region of the country, Bohemia, also makes its fair share of wines. Bohemia produces less wine than Moravia, yet it nevertheless provides a distinctive wine experience. North Prague, in the Mlnk wine area, is renowned for producing light-bodied white wines, particularly those made from the Müller-Thurgau grape. In this picturesque area, tourists can explore

vineyards, tour wineries, and partake in wine tastings.

You may anticipate a friendly and welcoming atmosphere when visiting Czech wine areas. Many vineyards have guided tours where you may discover more about the history of the area, grape management, and the winemaking process. You'll have the chance to sample a range of wines, from delicate reds to crisp whites, and learn about the distinctive qualities and flavors that Czech wines have to offer. Additionally, certain wineries host special occasions where you may fully experience the vibrant wine culture of the Czech Republic, like wine festivals and harvest festivities.

To learn more about the country's grape delights, whether you're a seasoned wine expert or you're just inquisitive about Czech wines, traveling the wine regions and indulging in tasting experiences is a pleasant way to do so. Raise a glass, take in the tastes, and salute the developing wine industry in the Czech Republic. Greetings and cheers!

Local Food Markets and Festivals

With a rich culinary history and a thriving food culture, the Czech Republic is a refuge for food lovers. Attending food festivals and wandering around markets are two of the best methods to get acquainted with the regional flavors and cuisine. The following major food events and markets may tempt your taste buds in the Czech Republic:

- Festival of Food in Prague: The Prague Food Festival, a prominent gourmet event showcasing the best of Czech and international food, is held yearly in the nation's capital. Famous chefs and eateries come together to serve their signature dishes, giving guests the chance to embark on a culinary journey. The event offers workshops, cooking demonstrations, food tastings, and a buzzing atmosphere full of foodies.
- Street Food Festival: If you enjoy street food, you must go to the Street Food Festival in Prague and other significant Czech cities. This exciting gathering of

food trucks and sellers offers a wide variety of regional and international street cuisine specialties. You can choose from a wide variety of flavors and culinary innovations, from gourmet burgers and tacos to traditional Czech snacks, to satiate your demands.
- Wine Festivals: The Czech Republic hosts several wine festivals all year long to honor the nation's long-standing winemaking heritage. One of the most well-liked occasions is the Mikulov Wine Festival in South Moravia, where you can savor a variety of regional wines, partake in wine tastings, and take in live music and cultural activities. Similar experiences are available at other wine festivals in various locales, such as the Znojmo Wine Festival and the Valtice Wine Festival.
- Farmers' Markets: Visiting a farmers' market is a great way to learn about the local cuisine and find fresh produce, handcrafted goods, and traditional Czech treats. Every Saturday, the Náplavka Farmers' Market in Prague is a crowded

place where you can discover a wide variety of regional fruits, vegetables, cheese, honey, baked products, and other things. Farmers' markets are also present in numerous cities and villages across the nation, providing an opportunity to interact with regional producers and enjoy their products.
- Easter markets: Around the Easter holiday, Czech cities and villages come alive with fun fairs selling regional delicacies and traditional Easter fare. The Old Town Square and Wenceslas Square Easter Markets in Prague are particularly well-liked. Beautifully adorned Easter eggs, gingerbread cookies, classic cakes, grilled sausages, and other festive treats are all available here.

You may interact with Czech culture, meet passionate food producers, and enjoy a variety of traditional and cutting-edge cuisine by attending these culinary festivals and touring the neighborhood markets. It's an opportunity to savor the local flavors, find undiscovered treasures, and make lifelong gastronomic memories. Come prepared to gratify your taste senses at these exquisite culinary festivals and markets in the Czech Republic by arriving with an empty stomach and an adventurous spirit.

CHAPTER 7

Cultural Events and Holidays

Discover the Czech Republic's abundant cultural legacy by visiting its historical sites, top-notch museums, alluring music and performing arts scene, and exciting traditional festivals. Experience the nation's diverse customs, creative outputs, and compelling cultural events to create lifelong memories.

Czech performing arts and music

Audiences have been mesmerized by the rich musical and performing arts legacy of the Czech Republic for many years. The nation is home to an abundance of talent and a thriving cultural scene, which includes both classical compositions and modern performances. Here are some examples of Czech performing arts and music's high points:

- The Czech Republic is frequently referred to as the "Land of Music," and with good cause. Numerous well-known composers, including Anton Dvoák, Bedich Smetana, and Leo Janáek, have called it home. The works of these artists are revered all over the world, and going to a classical music performance in Prague is a remarkable experience—especially at places like the Rudolfinum or the Estates Theatre.
- Prague National Theatre: The Prague National Theatre presents opera, ballet, and theater performances. It is a representation of Czech cultural identity. The world-class productions and gorgeous architecture make it a must-see for fans of the performing arts. Here, opera and ballet performances are celebrated for their superb artistry and compelling narratives.
- The Czech Philharmonic Orchestra is one of the most renowned orchestras in the world. The orchestra, which is renowned for its flawless musical interpretations and fervent performances, never ceases to enthrall audiences, both domestically

and abroad. A concert by the Czech Philharmonic offers the chance to experience music at its very best.
- Jazz and Current Music: There is a strong jazz and current music scene in the Czech Republic. The annual Prague Jazz Festival draws well-known jazz performers from all over the world, and jazz clubs and venues all around the nation provide a lively and personal atmosphere to take in live performances. The Czech music scene also includes a variety of musical styles, including electronic and alternative music as well as rock and pop.
- Theatre and puppetry are deeply ingrained cultural traditions in the Czech Republic. There are many theaters in Prague, including the venerable National Theatre and the Black Light Theatre, whose performances incorporate dance, music, and special effects. The legacy of puppetry in the nation is also honored, and puppet theatre presents captivating and distinctive performances for both kids and adults.

The Czech Republic offers a variety of venues for cultural excellence, including symphony halls, large opera houses, quaint jazz bars, and small theaters. The country's performing arts industry promises a musical voyage into cultural brilliance, whether you're a fan of modern compositions, contemporary compositions, or unique performances.

Local customs and attire

The lively folk traditions and distinctive clothing of the Czech Republic are deeply ingrained in the core of its cultural identity. These practices, which have been passed down through the decades, highlight the rich culture and traditions of the nation. A glimpse into the fascinating world of Czech folk customs and attire is provided below:
- Folk Festivals: Throughout the year, a variety of folk festivals are held throughout the Czech Republic, offering a vibrant stage for celebrating and maintaining long-standing traditions. These celebrations are a sensory extravaganza with vibrant parades,

powerful music, exuberant dances, and traditional attire. The International Folklore Festival in Prague and the Stránice Folklore Festival in Moravia are two of the most well-known events that draw performers from all over the world.

- Traditional Music and Dance: The preservation of the Czech Republic's cultural legacy is greatly aided by the folk music and dance of the country. The addictive rhythm that is created by folk dances like the polka and the czardas, backed by traditional instruments like the accordion and the fiddle, entices both residents and tourists to join in the fun. Traditional folk songs tell stories of love, nature, and daily life while frequently being sung in harmony, giving the Czech folk culture a melodic edge.
- Folk Costumes: The elaborate and exquisitely made folk costumes of the Czech Republic are well renowned. These clothes vary depending on the locale, reflecting certain regional traditions. The outfits are stunning to look at thanks to their elaborate embroidery, lacework,

and vibrant patterns. Embroidered shirts, waistcoats, and trousers are typical parts of men's costumes, whereas embroidered blouses, skirts, aprons, and headdresses are typical parts of women's costumes. These costumes demonstrate the expertise and pride of Czech artisans through their fine workmanship and attention to detail.

- Traditional Crafts: A vast variety of traditional crafts are included in Czech folk traditions. Pottery, glasswork, woodcarving, and lacework are just a few of the wonderful handicrafts produced by skilled artisans using age-old methods. These items are frequently displayed and offered for sale at neighborhood markets and craft fairs as a way to highlight the nation's rich artistic heritage.

You can dig into the traditions and tales that have influenced the Czech Republic's cultural fabric by investigating folk costumes and traditions. The Czech Republic's folk customs provide an enthralling window into its history and present, ranging from vibrant festivals and enthusiastic dances to intricately crafted costumes and traditional crafts. Give yourself over to experience the timeless beauty of the Czech Republic's cultural heritage and enter the enthralling realm of folk traditions.

Christmas celebrations and markets

The Czech Republic comes alive throughout the holiday season with gorgeous Christmas markets and happy festivals that take you into a winter paradise. These markets, which are brimming with sparkling lights, mouthwatering fragrances, and upbeat music, provide a singular opportunity to discover the mystique of Czech holiday customs. Here's a peek at the cheerful Czech Republic's Christmas markets and festivities:

- The Prague Christmas Markets, which transform the city's Old Town Square and Wenceslas Square into enchanted settings, is a highlight of the holiday season. Traditional handicrafts, ornaments, cozy woolen products, and delectable Czech fare are all available in wooden kiosks decked out for the holidays. Enjoy classic Czech treats like trdelnk while indulging in hot mulled wine (svaák), gingerbread biscuits (pernk), roasted chestnuts, and other treats.

- Regional Christmas Markets: The Czech Republic is home to several charming Christmas markets outside of Prague. A big Christmas tree and a wide variety of souvenirs and delicacies are available at the Brno Christmas Market, which is held in the city's main square. Olomouc, esk Krumlov, and other cities as well as Plzeň, both of which have wonderful markets with a festive ambiance and regional delicacies.
- Nativity Scenes: Making elaborate nativity scenes is one of the distinctive customs associated with Czech Christmas celebrations. These scenes, which are frequently seen in churches, chapels, and open areas, show the birth of Jesus Christ and the nearby characters. While some nativity scenes are intricate, with realistic figurines and small landscapes, others highlight the inventiveness of regional craftspeople.
- Advent Concerts and shows: Churches, music halls, and theaters feature a range of concerts and shows that honor the Christmas spirit during the Advent

season. These activities, which range from traditional folk performances to classical music concerts with renowned orchestras and choirs, encapsulate the spirit of the festive season and instill feelings of warmth and joy.

- Christmas Eve is a special time for Czech families, who get together to celebrate with a traditional Christmas dinner called "tdroveern veee," which typically consists of fish soup, fried carp with potato salad, mushroom dishes, and a variety of traditional sweets like honey cookies and fruit-filled pastries. This festive dinner being shared with loved ones is a treasured Czech Christmas custom.

You may immerse yourself in the warm traditions of the Czech Republic throughout the holiday season by visiting the Christmas markets and taking part in festive events. Make lasting memories of this magical time of year by allowing the dazzling lights, joyful music, and mouthwatering sweets to immerse you in the holiday spirit.

Easter traditions and celebrations

Easter is a treasured season in the Czech Republic when vivid celebrations and long-standing traditions combine to produce a singular and joyful celebration. Czech Easter customs offer a fascinating look into the nation's cultural legacy with their artistically painted Easter eggs, vibrant processions, and age-old folk rituals. Here's a peek into the vibrant world of Czech Easter traditions and celebrations:

- Decorating Easter eggs: Decorating Easter eggs is a crucial component of Czech Easter customs. Traditional methods are used to decorate intricately crafted eggs with vivid colors, elaborate designs, and meaningful themes. Like the "kraslice" technique in Moravia or the "drapank" technique in Bohemia, certain locations have their distinctive techniques. These exquisitely adorned eggs are seen as representations of fertility and new life.

- Easter Monday customs and traditions: Easter Monday, often referred to as "Velikonon pondl" in Czech, is a day full of unusual practices and rituals. One of the most well-known customs is "pomlázka," in which young guys amusingly lash girls on their legs with whips made from braided willow branches. This custom is said to bestow on the female's good health, beauty, and fortune. The girls give the lads colored eggs or ribbons in exchange.
- Easter Markets & Festivals: During Easter, several Czech cities and towns hold fun markets and activities. The traditional handicrafts, Easter-themed décor, and delectable foods available at these marketplaces are numerous. Handmade crafts artistically painted Easter eggs, and regional specialties including delicious pastries, honey products, and cakes shaped like lambs are also available.
- Processions and Religious Traditions: Easter is a significant religious holiday, and many towns and villages celebrate by

holding processions and other religious rituals. The most well-known of these is the "Whipping Procession" in the village of Ar nad Sázavou when participants act out the Stations of the Cross while costumed in traditional garb. These processions, which are accompanied by hymns and prayers, give citizens and guests the chance to see the country's deeply ingrained religious customs.

You may discover the lively customs and cultural diversity of the Czech Republic by immersing yourself in its Easter celebrations. Czech Easter traditions offer an enthralling trip into the heart of this festive season, from the beauty of Easter egg decorating to joyful processions and exuberant celebrations.

Film Festivals and Other Cultural Attractions

The Czech Republic is a center for artistic expression and love of culture, providing a dynamic backdrop for film festivals and other cultural events that draw viewers from near and far. The nation cherishes its rich cinematic legacy and presents a wide variety of creative manifestations, from prominent international film festivals to local celebrations of arts and culture. Here is a look at the Czech Republic's film festival and cultural event scene:

- The Karlovy Vary International Film Festival is one of the oldest and most well-known film festivals in Central Europe, drawing moviegoers, industry insiders, and filmmakers from all over the world. The festival, which takes place every year in the storied spa town of Karlovy Vary, features a large variety of foreign and Czech films, from cutting-edge indie productions to celebrated classics. It supports up-and-coming talent and honors the craft of cinematic storytelling.

- The Prague International Film Festival, usually referred to as Febiofest, is a well-known film event that presents a wide range of a collection of foreign movies, including dramas, comedies, and documentaries. The festival supports variety in the arts and promotes interaction between viewers and filmmakers. It provides an opportunity to examine current cinematic trends and find up-and-coming artists from around the world.
- The One World International Human Rights Documentary Film Festival is an important cultural occasion in the Czech Republic. Its mission is to raise awareness of human rights issues via the medium of documentaries. It offers films that make viewers think, tackling social, political, and environmental issues while encouraging societal change. The festival is held in numerous cities throughout the nation, enabling a larger audience to interact with these powerful stories.
- Despite not being a film festival, the Prague Spring International Music

Festival is still important to the culture and should be mentioned. World-class orchestras, well-known conductors, and outstanding players are all present at this renowned classical music festival for a series of spellbinding concerts. The festival emphasizes the beauty and depth of classical music, thrilling audiences with outstanding musical experiences in Prague's renowned concert halls, churches, and cultural venues.
- Local cultural festivals and festivities are also widely held in the Czech Republic, showcasing the nation's rich artistic past. Festivals of theater, musical performances, dance shows, and exhibitions presenting numerous artistic disciplines are some of these occasions. These regional events offer a look into the rich cultural tapestry of the Czech Republic, from the energetic Prague Fringe Festival to the Pilsen Cultural Summer.

You may commemorate the artistic accomplishments of both local and foreign talents in the Czech Republic by participating in film festivals and cultural events. A deeper understanding and appreciation for the cinematic arts and the many different cultural expressions that define our world are fostered by these events, which not only amuse but also inspire.

CHAPTER 8

Practical Advice and Safety Recommendations

Prepare to discover the wonders of the Czech Republic, a nation immersed in a vibrant culture, magnificent scenery, and rich history. There is something for everyone to discover, from the grand castles and quaint cobblestone alleyways to the lush forests and scenic countryside. As you set off on a memorable tour through this alluring location, let this guide be your traveling companion. Enjoy discovering the Czech Republic!

Information on health and safety

Your safety is our priority when visiting the Czech Republic. Here are some crucial health and safety advice to bear in mind for a safe and healthy journey:

- Make sure you have comprehensive travel insurance that covers medical situations before you leave. To ensure you have sufficient protection during your stay, familiarize yourself with the terms and coverage of your policy.
- Vaccinations: Before coming to the Czech Republic, find out from your doctor or a travel clinic if any shots are advised. Measles, mumps, and rubella (MMR) and tetanus-diphtheria-pertussis (Tdap) immunizations are common recommendations.
- Modern medical facilities are part of the Czech Republic's well-resourced healthcare system. Call 112 for quick assistance in an emergency, or go to the hospital or clinic that is closest to you. Carrying a list of crucial medical contacts and any relevant medical information is advised.

The Czech Republic is typically a safe place to visit, but it's vital to follow standard safety precautions. Keep an eye on your possessions, particularly when using public transportation or in crowded settings. Keep expensive stuff hidden, and be on the lookout for pickpockets. Always be on guard and mindful of your surroundings.

Keep in mind to stay hydrated, maintain proper hygiene, and abide by any local health recommendations or advice. You may have a worry-free and rewarding trip in the Czech Republic by putting your health and safety first.

Regional Customs and Protocol

Understanding and observing regional customs and etiquette will improve your cultural experience in the Czech Republic and make it easier for you to interact with the locals. To remember, have the following in mind:

- Greetings: It's polite to extend a solid handshake and make eye contact when meeting someone for the first time. Unless someone specifically requests it, use their title and last name when addressing them.

- Personal Space: Czechs treasure their privacy and frequently keep their distance when conversing. It's crucial to respect this line and refrain from approaching too closely or touching people without their consent.
- Politeness: In Czech culture, politeness is highly valued. It is polite to use the words "please" (prosm) and "thank you" (dkuji) when engaging with locals, employees, and vendors. Additionally, it's courteous to say hello to store owners and waiters when you enter and leave locations.
- Unless otherwise directed, it's customary to take your shoes off while entering someone's home. This promotes cleanliness and demonstrates consideration for the home.
- Public Conduct: Czechs place a high priority on quietness in public areas. In public transportation, museums, and other places where people congregate, refrain from shouting aloud or creating disturbances. In many indoor public locations, smoking is prohibited, and

designated non-smoking areas should be obeyed.
- Czechs typically dress neatly and conservatively, particularly for formal occasions or when visiting religious places. We appreciate modest dress and refrain from overly casual wear.

During your trip to the Czech Republic, you can make great interactions and lasting ties with the locals by adopting Czech customs and exhibiting respect for cultural traditions. Enjoy getting lost in this wonderful country's rich cultural tapestry!

Common Expressions and Czech Words

Even though many people in the Czech Republic understand English, learning a few fundamental Czech words might help you connect with locals and demonstrate respect while you're there. Here are some terms and phrases to know to get you where you need to go:

- Ahoj - Hello
- Prosím - Please
- Děkuji - Thank you
- Ano - Yes
- Ne - No
- Dobrý den - Good day
- Dobrou noc - Good night
- Ano - Yes
- Ne - No
- Promiňte - Excuse me
- Kde je...? - Where is...?
- Kolik to stojí? - How much does it cost?
- Jídlo - Food
- Voda - Water

- Pivo - Beer
- Restaurace - Restaurant
- Hotel - Hotel
- Nádraží - Train station
- Letiště - Airport
- Muzeum - Museum
- Banka - Bank
- Záchod - Toilet
- Autobus - Bus
- Tramvaj - Tram
- Vlak - Train
- Lístek - Ticket
- Pomoc - Help
- Bezpečnost - Safety
- Doprava - Transportation
- Hrad - Castle
- Promiňte, mluvíte anglicky? - Excuse me, do you speak English?
- Můžete mi prosím pomoci? - Can you please help me?
- Můžete mi ukázat na mapě? - Can you show me the map?
- Kde je nádraží? - Where is the train station?
- Kde je nejbližší bankomat? - Where is the nearest ATM?

- Kde mohu najít lékárnu? - Where can I find a pharmacy?
- Prosím, dám si jedno pivo. - Please, I'll have one beer.
- Mohu si objednat stůl pro dva? - Can I reserve a table for two?
- Mám rezervaci na jméno... - I have a reservation under the name...
- Jak se dostanu na letiště? - How do I get to the airport?
- Kde je nejbližší zastávka tramvaje? - Where is the nearest tram stop?
- Můžete mi dát jízdenku na jednu cestu do centra? - Can I have a one-way ticket to the city center, please?
- Kde je nejbližší toaleta? - Where is the nearest restroom?
- Chtěl bych objednat taxi. - I would like to order a taxi.
- Mohu platit kartou? - Can I pay by card?
- Kde se nachází nejlepší místa k vidění? - Where are the best places to visit?
- Můžete mi doporučit nějakou restauraci? - Can you recommend a restaurant?
- Co je to za specialitu? - What is this specialty?

- Mohu prosím dostat účet? - Can I have the bill, please?
- Co je toto? - What is this?
- Máte nějaký volný pokoj? - Do you have any available rooms?
- Jak se dostanu na Karlův most? - How do I get to Charles Bridge?
- Jak dlouho to trvá? - How long does it take?
- Můžete mi pomoci s mým zavazadlem? - Can you help me with my luggage?
- Kde je nejbližší turistické informační centrum? - Where is the nearest tourist information center?
- Máte Wi-Fi? - Do you have Wi-Fi?

Remember that even learning a few simple words and phrases in Czech would be appreciated by the locals and may make it easier for you to get by in everyday settings. During your visit to the Czech Republic, don't be scared to use and learn the language.

Buying goods and souvenirs

Discovering one-of-a-kind items and keepsakes that showcase the Czech Republic's rich culture and workmanship can be done by browsing the markets and stores there. These suggestions will help you have a better shopping experience:

- Popular Souvenirs: Handmade products like wooden toys, Bohemian crystals, delicate glassware, complex ceramics, marionettes, and vibrant traditional textiles are examples of typical Czech souvenirs. Find these genuine items to take home as souvenirs.
- Prague's Old Town and Lesser Town neighborhoods are home to a variety of stores and boutiques. Wenceslas Square is a well-known location for shopping. Discover hidden jewels and one-of-a-kind local businesses by exploring the smaller streets and districts.
- Christmas Markets: If you go during the holiday season, make sure to check out Prague's and other towns' enchanted Christmas markets. These joyous markets

provide a selection of handicrafts, holiday decorations, and regional foods.
- Genuine Czech Brands: Seek out reputable Czech brands that are renowned for their excellence and craftsmanship. Some well-known brands are Blue Prague for hand-painted ceramics, Bohemia Crystal for glassware, Manufaktura for natural skin care products, and Moser for the crystal.
- Visit open-air markets to locate locally produced goods, fresh fruit, handcrafted crafts, and vintage things as well as to take in the lively ambiance. One such well-known market worth seeing is the Havelská Market in Prague.
- Bargaining: In the majority of Czech shops, bartering is uncommon. However, especially in bigger stores or during the sale seasons, you might ask whether there are any ongoing specials or discounts.
- Tax-Free Shopping: If you're a visitor to the Czech Republic, you might be able to get your taxes back on some of the things you buy. To claim your return, look for

stores bearing the "Tax-Free" emblem and enquire about the procedure and required paperwork.
- Customs Regulations: To ensure compliance with any import limits or declarations, familiarize yourself with the customs regulations of your home nation before purchasing commodities like antiques, artwork, or cultural objects.

Check the store's refund and exchange policies and retain your receipts for warranty purposes. Enjoy the experience and take a piece of Czech culture home to treasure by shopping in the Czech Republic, where you may buy unique souvenirs and support local artists.

Traveling with Kids or Pets

Here are some suggestions to make your trip pleasurable and stress-free if you intend to travel to the Czech Republic with kids or bring along your pet friends:

Taking Kids on Vacation

- Accommodations: Seek out lodging options that welcome families and have features like play spaces, large rooms, and daycare services. Additionally, some hotels offer cribs or additional beds for kids.
- Activities and Attractions In ahead, do some research on family-friendly activities and attractions. A variety of alternatives are available in the Czech Republic, including interactive museums, parks, zoos, and adventure parks.
- Safety: Make sure your kids are safe by keeping them close in crowded places and teaching them the fundamentals of being safe. Learn the local hospitals' phone numbers and emergency contact information.

- Strollers & Baby Supplies: Strollers can be difficult to operate on Prague's cobblestone streets, so think about taking a lightweight stroller. Most shops and pharmacies have easy access to infant products like diapers and baby meals.
- Local Playgrounds: Make use of the numerous public playgrounds that are dispersed across the nation. These give kids a fantastic chance to let off steam and mingle with neighborhood kids.

Taking Pets on Vacation
- Pet-Friendly Accommodation: Search for lodging that allows animals. The Czech Republic has a large number of hotels and guesthouses that either feature pet-friendly rooms or accept pets for a fee.
- Pet regulations, such as those about documentation, vaccines, and microchipping, should be reviewed before bringing pets into the Czech Republic. Consult your veterinarian and the appropriate authorities in advance as each country's laws may differ.

- Pet-Friendly Transportation: Before using a public transportation system, become familiar with any applicable regulations. Larger dogs may need to be muzzled and on a leash, although small pets in carriers are frequently permitted on trams and buses.
- Pet-Friendly Parks and Outdoor Places: There are many parks and green places in the Czech Republic where you may walk and exercise your pet. Keep in mind to pick up after your pet and to abide by any leash or waste disposal laws that may be in effect in your neighborhood.
- Cafés and Restaurants That Accept Pets: In the Czech Republic, certain cafes and restaurants accept well-behaved pets in outside seating areas. To avoid any shocks, it's always a good idea to ask in advance.

Throughout your journey, keep in mind to put your children's and pets' comfort and safety first. Traveling in the Czech Republic with kids or dogs may be a pleasant experience with the right preparation and thought.

CHAPTER 9

Recommendations for Day Trips and Itineraries

Looking to go outside of the busy cities on your Czech adventure? Set out on fascinating day tours to find the nation's undiscovered gems. Discover Kutná Hora's historical allure, awe at the enchanted town of Esk Krumlov, or indulge in the therapeutic waters of Karlovy Vary's famed spas. These captivating locations provide visitors with a sense of Czech history, culture, and the country's stunning scenery. Pack your curiosity and go on a fascinating day tours to the Czech Republic to create lifelong experiences.

Day Trips from Prague

While Prague is a veritable museum of history and culture, the Czech Republic also has a wide range of fascinating day trip destinations that are close to the capital. Here are some

suggested day trips to improve your time in Prague:
- Karlštejn Castle is an exquisite fortress located just outside of Prague amid the lovely countryside. Discover the beautifully preserved medieval fortress, take in the breathtaking scenery, and delve into the fascinating past of this magnificent structure.
- Terezin Memorial: Pay your respects at the Terezin Memorial, a former Nazi concentration camp and ghetto during World War II. Visit the museum and memorial grounds to learn about this sad period in Czech history and to gain insight into the wartime experiences of captives.
- Český Krumlov: Travel to the quaint town of Esk Krumlov, a UNESCO World Heritage site, in the south. Explore its quaint cobblestone alleyways, awe at the medieval buildings, and go to the famous Esk Krumlov Castle. Don't forget to enjoy a relaxing boat trip along the Vltava River's meanders.

- Explore the fascinating town of Kutná Hora, which is renowned for its extensive history and stunning architecture. Admire the Gothic beauty of St. Barbara's Church and the Italian Court, as well as the astounding Sedlec Ossuary, which is decorated with thousands of human bones.
- Karlštejn Castle: Set out on a journey to the magnificent medieval fortification Karltejn Castle, which is situated amidst a lovely landscape. Visit the Chapel of the Holy Cross, see the castle's vast halls, and take in the expansive views of the surroundings.
- Discover the magnificent Konopiště Castle, which served as Archduke Franz Ferdinand of Austria's home. Learn about the castle's interesting history as you stroll through the picturesque gardens and admire the exquisitely decorated rooms.
- Bohemian Switzerland National Park: Bohemian Switzerland National Park, which is close to the German border, is a haven of unspoiled beauty. Hike through

magnificent landscapes covered with sandstone cliffs and lush forests as you take in the striking rock formations, investigate the alluring Pravická Gate, and marvel at them.

These day trips provide a wonderful chance to fully experience Czech history, culture, and natural splendors. These locations, whether you're interested in castles, historical sites, or magnificent scenery, will leave you with priceless memories.

Multi-day Routes for Country Exploration

If you have more time to visit the Czech Republic, think about setting out on multi-day journeys that will take you outside of the city and give you the chance to take in the variety of landscapes, historic monuments, and cultural riches that the nation has to offer. Here are some suggested routes to get you started on your Czech adventure:

- **South Bohemia, Esk Krumlov, and Prague (5-7 days)**

Explore the well-known landmarks and energetic neighborhoods of Prague first. Travel south to Esk Krumlov, where you may explore the historic castle and medieval-era town. Discover lovely villages like Tel, Trebon, and Ceske Budejovice as you continue to South Bohemia. Explore their stunning architecture and become fully immersed in the area's fascinating history.

- **Bohemian Spa Triangle: Prague, Karlovy Vary, and Karlovy Vary (4-6 days)**

Explore the historical sites, thriving culture, and breathtaking architecture of Prague to start. Visit Karlovy Vary, a posh resort town famous for its therapeutic thermal springs and elaborate colonnades. To complete the Bohemian Spa Triangle, proceed to Marianske Lazne and Frantikovy Lazn. Enjoy the peaceful environment, wellness services, and relaxation.

Six to eight days in Prague, Kutná Hora, and the Moravian Gems Explore Prague's historical and cultural attractions first. Travel to Kutná Hora to see the remarkable Sedlec Ossuary and learn more about the town's intriguing medieval past. Explore the dynamic city of Brno in Moravia and its architectural wonders, including Pilberk Castle and Villa Tugendhat.

Visit quaint villages like Mikulov and Lednice-Valtice, noted for their stunning châteaux and vineyards, as you tour the picturesque wine region of South Moravia.

- **A 5-7 day trip to Prague, Bohemian Switzerland, and Dresden**

Start in Prague, taking advantage of all that city has to offer in terms of history and culture.

Visit the Bohemian Switzerland National Park to explore the Pravická Gate, hiking trails, and unusual rock formations. Visit Dresden in Germany, a city renowned for its baroque architecture, top-notch museums, and the picturesque Elbe River.

These suggested itineraries give a taste of the varied attractions the Czech Republic has to offer, including historical gems, breathtaking natural features, and quaint towns. You are welcome to modify and alter them by your tastes and available time. Every region in Central Europe has a unique personality that makes it possible to plan a great trip there.

CHAPTER 10

Options for Accommodation

With a variety of lodging alternatives to suit every budget and preference, you'll be spoilt for choice when it comes to selecting the ideal place to stay during your trip to the Czech Republic. Here are a few well-liked options:

- Hotels: The Czech Republic has a vast selection of hotels, ranging from opulent 5-star establishments to welcoming boutique inns. Regardless of whether you want to stay in Prague or the lovely countryside, there are options available. For a variety of options, check websites like Booking.com or Expedia.
- Guesthouses and Bed and Breakfasts: Opt for a guesthouse or bed and breakfast for a more personal and cozy experience. These more intimate places can provide attentive service, cozy lodgings, and an opportunity to meet the local hosts.

- Holiday Apartments & Vacation Rentals: Having your own space gives you more freedom and independence, so renting a holiday apartment or vacation home is a terrific choice. You may experience the Czech Republic as a local by using websites like Airbnb, HomeAway, and VRBO, which provide a large range of houses throughout the nation.
- Hostels: They provide economical lodging in communal dormitories or individual rooms, making them the perfect choice for sociable travelers on a tight budget. Hostels in the Czech Republic are widely preferred by backpackers and lone travelers because they frequently include social spaces, kitchens, and planned activities.
- Consider staying at an agritourism facility or farm stay for a distinctive rural experience. With these lodgings, you can experience rural life up close, eat meals straight from the farm, and take part in rural pursuits like wine tasting and animal feeding.

- Campgrounds: If you love being outside, camping can be a great option. There are many campgrounds in the Czech Republic, ranging from modest sites with necessary services to well-equipped establishments with recreational activities. Camping offers an affordable lodging option and lets you enjoy the nation's natural splendor.

When selecting a place to stay, take into account aspects like location, amenities, reviews, and accessibility to amenities or transit. It is advisable to make reservations in advance, particularly during busy travel times or for well-known locations like Prague. The Czech Republic offers a wide variety of lodging options that will help you feel at home during your stay, regardless of your preferences or budget.

Tour Guides and Transportation Services

Consider using tour companies and transportation services that provide practical solutions and knowledgeable advice to make your trip to the Czech Republic simple and pleasurable. Here are a few suggestions:

- Trains, buses, trams, and metros are all part of the Czech Republic's well-developed public transit network. Regional buses and trams offer easy transportation within cities and towns, while Czech Railways (eské dráhy) runs train services linking major cities. The vast metro system in Prague makes getting about the capital city simple.
- Private transfer services are offered if you want a more individualized and hassle-free travel experience. These services offer comfortable and convenient door-to-door transportation between airports, cities, and tourist attractions. Prague Airport Transfers and Czech Shuttle, for example, provide dependable private travel solutions.

- Renting a car allows you the flexibility to discover the Czech Republic at your speed. You can pick up a vehicle at airports, train stations, or metropolitan locations across the nation, which is serviced by major international car rental firms. However, keep in mind that parking in city centers might be scarce and expensive.
- Guided Tours: If you want to make the most of your stay in the Czech Republic and learn from experienced guides, think about going on a guided tour. City tours, day trips, cultural excursions, and themed experiences are just a few of the alternatives provided by tour companies like Viator, GetYourGuide, and Czech Tours. These tours offer enlightening commentary, front-of-the-line entry to sights, and the chance to interact with other tourists.
- Outdoor adventure tours can be arranged by tour companies that specialize in outdoor pursuits including hiking, cycling, and kayaking. These excursions can be taken in the Czech Republic's

scenic areas and national parks. For outdoor enthusiasts, businesses like Active Czech provide specialized itineraries and equipment rentals.

- River Cruises: Take a riverboat down the Vltava River to see the Czech Republic's natural beauty from a new angle. Numerous tour companies provide cruises that highlight the nation's breathtaking vistas, including Prague's well-known riverside attractions.

When choosing transportation providers or tour operators, take into account aspects like reputation, client feedback, cost, and the variety of services provided. It's a good idea to make reservations in advance, especially for popular trips or during the busiest travel times.

Printed in Great Britain
by Amazon

30180229R00086